Praise for *Brian K. Allen & I*

"I took the security management course and criminal profiling course. Both were very informative, and the correspondence was quick and easy! I enjoyed the courses and plan on taking more!"

~ Christopher Martinez

"Hi Brian, The courses: "Criminal Profiling", "Criminal Investigator", "Crime Scene Investigations" were very useful to me and helped me to upgrade new knowledge and skills. It is very well organized and meaningful. Thank you!"

~ Ralitsa Sartsanova

Praise for *Brian K. Allen & International Security Training, LLC*

"The field of security, investigation, and protective services is one that I've enjoyed to have as a fall back to my career in management and my responsibilities in leadership throughout my years of employment. Having grown up in a family with career law enforcement and military professionals; the challenges of the profession are not new to me. What is new, exciting, and refreshing is the approach to the simplification and the ease of material presentation that enables both the experienced and novice alike to learn with efficiency; making the study lessons both a condensed and yet an effective delivery of coursework. During my years of field work; on many occasions I heard the expression: "Good Intelligence is one that field agents can assimilate, and disseminate, in order to effectively inform in a simplified format that facilitates the understanding of complex facts on hand, and enables us to make rational and sound derisions even under duress." With this being made clear; it is my personal perception that Director Brian K. Allen, has accomplished this with the courses that he offers through International Security Training, L.L.C. I am impressed and highly recommend the courses to everyone interested in this field of work."

~ Joseph G Guedea

InternationalSecurityTraining.org

Top Secret Security Information That Higher Paid Security Specialists Know and Minimum Wage Security Guards Don't!

Edition 162261

InternationalSecurityTraining.org

This Page Intentionally Left Blank

InternationalSecurityTraining.org

Copyright Page

Copyright © 2019 / Edition 162261 – Brian K. Allen

Cover Design © 2018 – Brian K. Allen

All rights reserved. No part of this publication may be reproduced or transmitted in any form or by any means, including informational storage and retrieval systems, without permission in writing from the copyright holder, except for brief quotations in a review.

ISBN-13:   978-1537085739

ISBN-10:   1537085735

First Printing, August 2016

Dedication

This book is dedicated to the men and women who gave their lives while serving in the US Armed Forces. I was lucky enough to come home from my deployment and I'll never forget those who did not. Rest in peace brothers and sisters.

Would You Mind Leaving A Review?

After reading this book, if you find that the information shared is what was promised in the Table of Contents… please leave a review on Amazon.com & Barnes and Noble. Thank you!

Acknowledgements

To my parents, Ken D. Allen & Marilyn L. Ward (Barber). It's because of your love, support, and comforting words in the most difficult times that I learn from my mistakes and have even had a few successes. ☺

To all my students, past, present, and future, who have allowed me to shape their professional development. Without you, I wouldn't be in business.

To all of my supervisors, managers, coaches, trainers, and mentors (civilian & military). This book is a culmination of all the notes I've taken while learning from and working under you. I didn't invent or discover any of the information in this book. I learned it from all of you. I hope by sharing my notes and experiences, I help improve the professional security industry.

Table of Contents

Part One	YOU: The Security Specialist	13
Chapter 1......	Enhanced Professionalism	15
Chapter 2......	Verbal De-escalation	25
Chapter 3......	Understanding Body Language	41
Part Two	The Physical Security Industry	51
Chapter 4	Fundamentals of Physical Security	53
Chapter 5	Casino Security	111
Chapter 6	Conclusion	165
Resources & Bibliography		167
About the Author		169
Online Courses Available		171

Part 1: YOU – The Security Specialist

In this part, we focus on the human being. First, you - the security specialist and second, the people you'll come into contact with. We feel this is the most important area to focus on when someone tells us they want to perform and be recognized in Top 10 Percent of the industry.

This industry is very competitive. There are many people with military and law enforcement backgrounds who are competing for high level jobs and/or contracts. The majority have great looking resumes and career experience. The "soft skills" are what will propel you – above them – when everything else is equal.

So, learn about yourself, other people, and communication in part one!

Chapter 1: Enhanced Professionalism

You learn far more from negative leadership than from positive leadership. Because you learn how not to do it. And, therefore, you learn how to do it.
~Norman Schwarzkopf

A couple times a year, you can find stories where a person started somewhere as a security guard earning minimum wage and was quickly promoted to a management position earning a great salary. You'll also be able to find stories of people who've been bodyguards for a client and then promoted to high salary positions in completely different departments. We can look at this in two ways.

First, we can say it's unfortunate that situations like these are the exception, rather than the norm. Second, we can study the people that do get the promotions and learn what separates them from the majority of folks. Since the second way is more proactive, that's what we did. We discovered that when resumes and educational backgrounds were equal, the one area that caused the few to get promoted ahead of the majority, was **enhanced professionalism**.

Seems common sense, but knowing and doing are two different things. So are the results. The benefits of being professional at work include raises, promotions, and the respect from your co-workers. Sometimes it's difficult to remain professional every hour of the day, we get it. However, it gets easier when you make professionalism a habit. **Focus on your own performance** (not other co-workers) and you'll start to see the rewards of your hard work.

Napoleon Hill once wrote that *"if you do more than you're paid to do today, one day you'll be paid more than for what you do."* Let's look at enhanced professionalism from two different aspects, behaviors & attributes.

Behaviors

1. Be on time in the morning and all day.

If your starting time is 6:00 a.m., then be in your office / post no later than 5:45 a.m. If your lunch hour starts at noon, then make it a point to be back in the office **working** by 1:00 p.m. every single day. Make it a habit to always be on time. Don't be the person that always creates stress in the people you're relieving because you clock in "on the dot" and don't relieve them for another 15 minutes.

2. Become a resource to the people you work with.

Pay attention in departmental meetings and be sure to read the company memos that circulate through the website and in the company mailbox. If you stay on top of company information, then people will recognize you as a resource and respect your professional approach to your job. 80% of employees ignore / trash the company newsletter. This is not for you. You are the enhanced professional.

3. Avoid office politics and gossip.

It's an unfortunate truth that workplace politics & rumors is a way of life for the majority of employees. But if you avoid office drama and stay far away from co-worker gossip, then you'll establish the professional reputation you want. Never feed into the line staff vs management, noncommissioned soldiers vs officers, or minimum wage vs wealthy people battles. If you're reading this book, we assume you're not wanting to be average. Average people will always do those things. Let your results & achievements speak louder than your words.

4. Dress professionally.

When it comes to dressing professionally, you don't need to wear a business suit every day. Your job came with a dress code and you need to follow that code. If your job requires a business formal dress code, then follow it. Keep yourself professionally groomed, and always pay attention to your personal hygiene. Don't push the boundaries or become a headache for management. This won't get you outstanding annual reviews, raises, or promotions.

5. Show respect for others in your office.

You don't need to be the shoulder everyone cries on, but you do need to have respect for others and show common courtesy to your co-workers. If there's a fellow employee that you'd rather not associate with, then avoid their company but don't get involved in whispering behind their back. You never know who they know or are related to. You don't have to be friends but you don't have to be enemies either.

6. Always follow company policies.

Most companies create an employee handbook that outlines the policies and procedures you should follow. Carefully review this manual and make sure you're getting your job done efficiently and to code. Use company policies as your framework for how you perform your job. You may not like some of the polices. Who cares?! They're not paying you to like anything.

7. Get your job done.

Texting, taking phone calls and the internet make it easy to get sidetracked and lose sight of your deadlines. But when you're trying to be more professional at work, you need to stay focused on your job and remain productive. Create a task list that you follow every day, and avoid the kinds of distractions that cause you to lose sight of your responsibilities. You don't have to answer every call – let it go to voicemail. Return the call when you have the privacy needed.

8. Carry a notepad with you to write down important info.

As you walk down the hall at work, a manager stops you and asks you to take care of a quick task for him. You agree to it and then get back to your desk, but didn't write it down. The next morning, the manager informs you that he'll have to work this weekend to complete the task that you completely forgot about. This make you look unreliable.

Whether it's a digital notepad or an old-fashioned pen and paper, professionals carry something with them to write down important tasks and make sure they get done.

9. Never be afraid to ask questions.

Professionals are eager to learn new things, but they also want to clearly understand what's expected of them. You need to ask questions and then use the information you get to improve your career. That being said, timing and environment are something to pay attention to. Ask, but at the most appropriate time.

10. Look forward to each day.

A professional looks forward to the opportunities and challenges that each new day brings. You shouldn't dread going to work every morning - instead, savor the opportunity to learn and grow on a daily basis. Easier said than done, we know. Just do the very best you can in this effort.

Attributes

1. Confidence

Confidence without the ability to back it up is useless, but if you're truly competent, own it. You don't have to be aggressive either. Quiet confidence is a great thing to have.

2. Candor

Truly professional people are forthright. They assess the situation, calculate the risks, and offer a truthful opinion. Again, timing and environment should be taken into consideration.

3. Self-awareness

This is a part of displaying confidence -- knowing who you are and where you fit in the world, and owning your strengths and weaknesses. If you do that, you can work to buttress the things you don't do as well.

4. Strategic thinking

One of the basic tenets of success is to 'start with the end in mind'. Truly professional people identify their goals, then work backward to achieve them.

5. Anticipation

Know that focusing on others' needs to the point that you can anticipate their challenges and solutions, breeds confidence. If you make other people look good *in addition to yourself*, you have developed enhanced professionalism.

6. Caring

Related to anticipation: You can't truly help others if you can't bother to learn about their goals and fears. The reward will come. Maybe not from **this** employer but it will come from somewhere. As the saying goes, *"your reputation precedes you"*.

7. Follow-through & Diligence

Say you'll do something, then do it. Keep people informed of statuses. It keeps them calm and reduces unexpected phone calls or office drop-ins to see where things are at. Be persistent, demonstrate worth ethic, and "check the small things."

9. Enthusiasm

Gen. Colin Powell put it best: Perpetual optimism is a force multiplier. Don't be fake, but saying "our results will be better than our circumstances predict" is professional enthusiasm.

10. Discretion

Caring and self-awareness, combined with good communications ability, leads to prudence and the ability to be candid without giving offense.

11. Humor

You don't need to be hilarious, but you need a sense of humor; it demonstrates perspective.

12. Fitness

This is unfortunate but true. If someone looks as if he or she doesn't care about their health, it's a lot harder to project professionalism -- and with it, the notion that they care about other things.

So, there we have it! A collection of behaviors and attributes that when employed, will communicate **enhanced professionalism** to all who observe. In a society where entitlement seems to precede earning… where claiming discrimination / victimization precedes personal accountability… this chapter can set you far ahead of your competition.

Chapter 2: Verbal De-escalation

For to win one hundred victories in one hundred battles is not the acme of skill. To subdue the enemy - without fighting - is the acme of skill.

~Sun Tzu

Legal & Ethical Reasons For Tactical Verbal De-escalation

The first and most important reason for this topic = Safety for you and your partner(s)! The most dangerous weapon you have, is your snappy response, after being angered. One wrong word could get you:

1. Shot, stabbed or killed on the job
2. Fired or ruin your reputation

    a. Bad habits can create smoke around your name. That smoke becomes a jacket and that jacket, becomes a ruined career.

The second reason is "Enhanced Professionalism" for the Security & Law Enforcement profession. We need to be good at our jobs. Being right, is an obvious part of our job, but only part of it. We also need to look good. We are being watched & evaluated all the time. Add in sounding good, as well. Same reasons as mentioned above.

The third reason, fewer complaints. This should be self-explanatory. Fourth, we have vicarious liability. One of the newest occupations out there is suing people, agencies and companies. Unfortunately, there are people out there who'd rather sue you or your employer, rather than work for a living or improve themselves so that they can have a better life.

For this reason, the **problem officer / operator** is no longer tolerated in our industry or anywhere else. The fifth reason is less personal stress. This industry has enough stress as it is, there is no good reason for adding in more.

The Bottom Line

Interact with the client's customers (internal & external) and/or bad guys professionally. That's what our employer wants, so that's what we'll do! What is the main goal of professional security & law enforcement? The goal is to generate voluntary compliance and prevent any incidents that could harm the client / community.

The reason Voluntary Compliance is difficult these days, is because we are a world of people who love these three questions:

1. Why do I have to?
2. What gives you the right to tell me? (*Challenging your authority*)
3. What's in it, for me?

Your 3 Immediate Goals =

Keeping Tempers Down - Persuading Folks - Solving Problems

One Of The Top Professions

Let's review 7 reasons why we feel law enforcement & security are arguably, among the top professions on the planet.

1.) High visibility

> We've lost the right to be out of shape. We have to be able to defend ourselves. Our families depend on us to come home safely. (Familial and financial reasons)

> Bottom line: If you're not trying to consistently improve your fitness, your family may have to bear a burden, which you could have prevented. If you're seriously injured or killed on duty, being in good shape will thwart comments like, "what do you expect, they haven't been in shape since the

Academy". Remember, our partners depend on us to assist in defending them.

We've lost the right to speak as we feel while at work. While on the job, we have to perform as a professional, despite our personal feelings, opinions or prejudices.

2.) Life & Death Decisions

In the security & law enforcement arena, we have to respond not only to the criminal threat, but also the emergency situations that may arise. (Fires, HazMat Spills, Workplace Violence, etc.) We have to make decisions in these situations in a split second.

3.) Codified Body of Knowledge

The people who work in our industry must have knowledge in the following areas, at a minimum:

a. Security / Law Enforcement Professional Fundamentals
b. OSHA / Equiv. Requirements
c. Emergency First Aid Skills
d. Conflict Resolution Skills
e. Workplace Violence Recognition & Prevention

4.) Continuous Training

We have to go through initial and refresher training in areas such as:

- New Communication Techniques (Verbal & Non-verbal)
- Electronic Security Equipment
- Principles of Protection
- Threat recognition
- Company advancements and procedural changes
- and much more

5.) Adaptability to change

We have to accept and appreciate the fact that change can occur on a very frequent basis. Changes in areas such as:

- General Security Requirements
- Procedural / Response Changes Following Incidents
    - Each incident shall be evaluated to see if any changes in officer response can be made to improve the safety of all people involved.

- These evaluations need to be looked at as an opportunity to grow and not as personal criticism aimed at the security staff involved.

6.) Ethical Standards of Conduct

Being that part of our job is to enforce certain standards & laws, we must happily follow them ourselves. Gone is the day where we were lax in the enforcement of rules, until we were caught ourselves.

This has been the mark of the unprofessional security / police officer of the past. One that would say something like, "Now that I've been busted and have to straighten up, just wait and see how tough I am on the other people!"

7.) Must be licensed

Obviously for security work - each country, state, province, etc. has different laws. But the bottom line still remains... we exist to protect the personnel, property and information of our client. For police, add in protection of the community. That's a huge responsibility.

As an officer, the authority granted to you by the client or local government, is one of complete trust. There is no room for an officer to be part of the problem. We must become part of the solution!

Force Continuum

When can you use deadly force? Only when you're in imminent jeopardy! This means the bad guy has the below items manifested to either kill you or cause great bodily harm:

1. Intent
2. Ability
3. Means
4. Opportunity

Now, even if the bad guy has all the above items in place, does this give you blanket authority to use deadly force? Not necessarily. Only if you can show **preclusion**!

Questions regarding preclusion that you could be asked by a supervisor or attorney include:

- Did you have to use deadly force?
- Could you have simply run away?
- Was the confrontation unavoidable?
- Did you use all force options available? If no, why not?

Force Options

1. Professional Presence

We must look interested in all incidents and services for our client, even when we're really not.

- 6th traffic stop of the day
- 27th employee loaner badge of the day
- 19th phone call asking about the "such & such" incident

We must gain "Mastery through Adaptation" & Street Savvy. Those include the ability to become who you have to be, in order to effectively handle the situation/person in front of you."

- Flexibility & adaptability is a must

2. Verbal Commands & De-escalation Skills

3. Empty Hand Control / Pain compliance

- For most security officers, this means **self-defense** only. Most security staff do not protect property by physically restraining the bad guy. If an incident occurs like this, the security staff involved will have to justify their actions and be prepared for some hard questioning by management.

- Obviously, law enforcement has more responsibility and other reasons to validate going hands-on.

4. Less Lethal (Pepper spray, stun guns, tasers)

- Training must be completed for the specific item, prior to being allowed to carry and use.

5. Impact Weapons (Club/Baton)

- The same considerations mentioned for #3 above, apply here.

6. Deadly Force

- Self-Defense or protection of a third party only! See the "When can you use deadly force" section above!

Some security employees ask, "Why should I pay attention to this force option stuff when I know that 99% of the time nothing will happen here?"

- Answer: We train & prepare for the 1% when something will happen.

Creating A De-escalation Mindset

We want you to develop a new "Habit of Mind". The ancient samurai used to teach: Mushin = No Mind" or "No Bias". A modernized translation = Dis-interested / Un-biased.

We are hired to help solve the problem... not to display an opinion about it. We need to understand that flexibility does not show softness or weakness. Instead, it shows true power & strength. Consider the strength of the Willow Tree. After a tornado, it is oftentimes the only tree left unharmed. Or, how about the re-curve bow? The further you bend it back, the more strength it gains.

Develop Your Verbal Responses Ahead Of Time

We should always realize in advance, that people we're dealing with in police or security work, will insult us verbally or speak to us in a disrespectful manner. Unfortunately, it's human nature.

An old samurai warrior once said... "When man throw spear, move head!" When referring to verbal abuse, that phrase is a lot better than "sticks and stones may break my bones but names will never hurt me!"

Why? Because for 90% of us, that's not true! Verbal abuse hurts / angers us, even when we hide it. Never let someone draw you into an argument! You're stronger and more professional than that. When someone cusses you out or is verbally attacking you or the rules, try these deflectors:

- I preciate that but...
- I unerstan' that but...
- I hear that but...
- I got that but...
- I believe that but...
- Make up your own deflector statements!

Ask someone senior to you, what verbal taunts are commonly used against them... in their working day. Write those down. Then ask them what verbal response they like to use, when trying to deflect the comment and de-escalate the situation.

Imagine asking 5 or 10 veteran officers this. You could end up having 15 – 20 of the most common verbal attacks AND professional responses.

Sales people do this! They have a script that has replies to each objection a potential buyer may throw at them. This process works!

By using verbal deflectors, I want you to:

1. Feel good (Your partner knows you're in control)
2. Dis-empower the bad guy
3. Sound good in these three areas

- Street / In Public
- Court
- Media

Follow these three principles when dealing with a bad guy or difficult person:

1. Say what you want... do as I say.

Unless it presents an officer safety problem or is riotous.

2. Since you have the last act, let them have the last word!

Remember, they are competing for the attention of the audience. Just like YOU need to Be Good, Look Good, and Sound Good - so does the bad guy. Since he's in trouble, he can't be good. Since he's going to jail, he can't look good. So go ahead and let him LOOK GOOD in front of all his friends by mouthing off.

3. Learn: RE-spect v.s. Respect

- Understanding this will make you a better officer.
    - It means:
        - Hold me accountable for my actions
        - Do so without verbal abuse or disrespect.
        - Treat me, as you'd expect to be treated, under identical circumstances.

Become A Contact Professional

Let's look at the word contact:

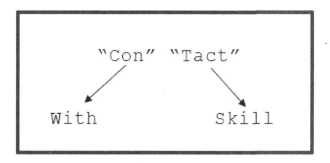

First, we need to be in CONTACT with ourselves! At home today, write down five or six of your communication weaknesses or prejudices.

1.
2.
3.
4.
5.
6.

Remember, always hide your triggers / buttons. We all have some.

Then, we need to be in CONTACT with our employer. Who do we represent???

- company
- ceo
- security department
- security industry
- Constitution and Bill of Rights / or equivalent

Let's start taking pride in:

1. WHO we represent

2. Our profession

Study the graphic below:

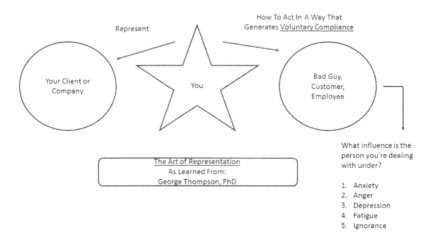

How do our negative comments, threats, and insults contribute to Voluntary Compliance? They don't! They may make us feel better, temporarily – but that's all. Ineffective communication does not solve problems or generate voluntary compliance.

Remember, as law enforcement or safety/security officers we are just a voice, a medium. A medium that represents our employer. Don't show your ego and loudly threaten to swing a big hammer. Stay balanced!

If you work outside the above graphic, in any way, you will lose:

1. Power
2. Leadership

The more ego you can get rid of, the more power you'll have over people.

Let's wrap this chapter up. Remember, common sense is highly uncommon under pressure! Our job is to Bring PEACE out of discord! I want you to think of yourself as a contact professional, who from the beginning, WILL control the situation. Respond to people, never react! "Respond" suggests that you Re-answer. "Re-act" suggests that you're being controlled from the outside. Also - take pride in your ability to bend and flex... looking for voluntary compliance... working toward better communication. Finally, remember, it's not good enough to **be** Good! You've also got to **look good** and **sound good** or... it's no good!

Chapter 3: Understanding Body Language

The most important thing in communication is hearing what isn't said.
~Peter F. Drucker

Noticing Signs of Comfort or Discomfort

When you're observing someone's behavior, look for physical signs of comfort and discomfort. I learned this from a former FBI agent named Joe Navarro. Two common signs of comfort are the smile and the head tilt. Four signs of discomfort include touching the neck, squinting the eyes, pressing the lips – making them disappear, and moving the forehead.

This chapter will focus on body language as it pertains to security and law enforcement work. That being said, I want you to keep Joe Navarro's fundamental philosophies of comfort & discomfort as the main indicator of how a person is feeling, thinking or trying to appear. One review I found online stated the following:

"The fundamental premise behind Navarro's work is that our nonverbal behavior indicates one of two states: comfort or discomfort. When we are enjoying a conversation, feel positive about

an interaction, or are interested in a topic, we may tilt our heads, move closer to the other person, or give a relaxed smile. If we are uncomfortable with the conversation, or feel uncertainty, fear, defensiveness, or anger, we may engage in "blocking" motions such as crossing our arms or legs, tighten our jaw muscles, or involuntarily squint our eyes slightly and quickly."

Comfort & discomfort... ok, what about signs of interest or boredom? Interest can be indicated through posture or extended eye contact, such as standing and listening properly. Boredom is often shown by the head tilting to one side, or by the eyes looking straight at the speaker but becoming slightly unfocused. "Zoning out" has happened to most of us.

Misreading signs: A head tilt may indicate a sore neck, trust or even a feeling of safety! (Part of the neck becomes uncovered, hence vulnerable.) Did you know it's virtually impossible to tilt our head in front of someone we don't trust or are scared of? As for the eyes... unfocused eyes may indicate ocular problems in the listener. As you can imagine, many times people who had tilted their heads and appeared to be zoning out were actually having the above mentioned issues.

Sincerity and Deceit

Looking for Incongruent Behaviors

If someone's words do not match their nonverbal behaviors, you should pay careful attention. For example, someone might tell you they are happy while frowning and staring at the ground. Research has shown that when words fail to match up with nonverbal signals, people tend to ignore what has been said and focus instead on unspoken expressions of moods, thoughts, and emotions.

Non-Verbal

Look for micro-expressions. Micro-expressions are facial expressions that flash on a person's face for a fraction of a second and reveal the person's true emotion, underneath the lie. Some people may be naturally sensitive to them but almost anybody can train themselves to detect these micro-expressions.

Typically, in a person who is lying, his or her micro-expression will be an emotion of distress, characterized by the eyebrows being drawn upwards towards the middle of the forehead, causing short lines to appear across the skin of the forehead.

Look for nose touching and mouth covering. People tend to touch the nose more when lying and a great deal less when telling the truth. This is perhaps due to a rush of adrenaline to the capillaries in the nose, causing the nose to itch. A lying person is more likely to cover his or her mouth with a hand or to place the hands near the mouth, almost as if to cover the lies coming forth. If the mouth appears tense and the lips are pursed, this can indicate distress.

Notice the person's eye movements. You can usually tell if a person is remembering something or making something up based on eye movements. When people remember details, their eyes move up and to the left if they are right-handed. When right-handed people make something up, their eyes move up and to the right. The reverse is true of left-handed people. People also tend to blink more rapidly ("eye flutter") as they're telling a lie. More common in men than in women, another sign of a lie can be rubbing the eyes.

Watch the eyelids. These tend to close longer than the usual blink when a person sees or hears something he or she doesn't agree with. However, this can be a very minute change, so you will need to know how the person blinks normally during a non-stressful situation for accurate comparison. If the hands or fingers also go to the eyes, this may be another indicator of trying to "block out" the truth.

Be careful about assessing the truthfulness of someone's statement based on eye movements alone. Recent scientific studies have cast doubt on the idea that looking a certain direction can help pinpoint someone who is lying. Many scientists believe that eye directionality is a statistically poor indicator of truthfulness.

Do not use eye contact or lack of it as a sole indicator of truthfulness. Contrary to popular belief, a liar does not always avoid eye contact. Humans naturally break eye contact and look at non-moving objects to help them focus and remember. Liars may deliberately make eye contact to seem more sincere; this can be practiced to overcome any discomfort, as a way of "proving" that truth is being told.

Indeed, it has been shown that some liars tend to increase the level of eye contact in response to the fact that investigators have often considered eye contact as a clue. Clearly, only use eye contact aversion as one indicator in a general context of increasing distress when being asked difficult questions.

Check for sweating. People tend to sweat more when they lie. Actually, measuring sweat is one of the ways that the polygraph test (the "lie detector" in all the movies) determines a lie. Yet again, taken on its own, this is not always a reliable indication of lying. Some people may sweat a lot more just because of nervousness, shyness or a condition that causes the person to sweat more than normal. It's one indicator to be read along with a group of signs, such as trembling, blushing and difficulty in swallowing.

Watch when the person nods. If the head is nodding or shaking in opposition to what is being said, this can be a clue. This is called "incongruence." For example, a person might say that he or she did something, such as "I cleaned those pots thoroughly" while shaking the head "no", revealing the truth that the pots were wiped briefly but not scrubbed. Unless a person is trained well, this is an easy unconscious mistake to make and such a physical response is often the truthful one.

Also, a person may hesitate before nodding when giving an answer. A truthful person tends to nod in support of a statement or answer at the same time it is being given; when someone is trying to deceive, a delay may occur.

Watch out for fidgeting. A sign that someone is lying is that they fidget, either with their own body or with random things around them. Fidgeting results from nervous energy produced by a fear of being found out. In order to release the nervous energy, liars often fidget with a chair, a handkerchief, or a part of their body.

Observe the level of mirroring. We naturally mirror the behavior of others with whom we're interacting; it's a way of establishing rapport and showing interest. When lying, mirroring may drop as the liar spends a lot of effort on creating another reality for the listener. Some examples of failed mirroring that might alert you that something's not right, follow below.

Leaning away. When a person is telling the truth or has nothing to hide, he or she tends to lean toward the listener. On the other hand, a liar will be more likely to lean backward, a sign of not wanting to give more information than is necessary. Leaning away can also mean dislike or disinterest.

In people telling the truth, head movements and body gestures tend to be mirrored as part of the interplay between the speaker and the listener. A person trying to deceive may be reluctant to do this, so signs of not copying gestures or head movements could indicate an attempt to cover up. You might even spot a deliberate action to move a hand back to another position or to turn a different way.

Watch the person's throat. A person may constantly be trying to lubricate their throat when they lie by swallowing, gulping or clearing their throat. Lying causes their body to increase production of adrenaline, which gets their saliva pumping and then creates very little. While the saliva is surging, the subject might be gulping it down. When the saliva is no longer surging, the subject might be clearing their throat.

Check the person's breathing. A liar tends to breathe faster, displaying a series of short breaths followed by one deep breath. The mouth may appear dry (causing much throat clearing). Again, this is because they are putting their body through stress, which causes the heart to beat faster and the lungs to demand more air.

Notice the behavior of other body parts. Watch the person's hands, arms and legs. In a non-stressful situation, people tend to be comfortable and take up space by being expansive in hand and arm movements, perhaps sprawling their legs comfortably. In a lying person, these parts of the body will tend to be limited, stiff, and self-directed. The person's hands may touch his or her face, ear, or the back of the neck. Folded arms, interlocked legs and lack of hand movements can be a sign of not wanting to give away information.

Liars tend to avoid hand gestures that we consider a normal part of discussion or conversation. With some caveats, most liars will avoid finger pointing, open palm gestures, stippling (fingertips touching each other in a triangle shape often associated with thinking out loud), etc.

Check the knuckles. Liars who stay motionless may grip the sides of a chair or other object until the knuckles turn white, not even noticing what's happening. Grooming behaviors are common in liars, such as playing with hair, adjusting a tie, or fidgeting with a shirt cuff.

Two caveats to remember:

Liars can deliberately slouch to appear "at ease". Yawning and bored behavior may be a sign of trying to act just a little casual about the situation so as to cover up deception. Just because they're at ease doesn't mean they're not lying.

Keep in mind that these signals may be a sign of nervousness and not a sign of deceit. The subject in question might not necessarily be nervous because they're lying.

Signs of Conflict

Conflict is not always physical. 'Disbelief' or 'non-agreement' is often indicated by an averted gaze, or by touching the ear or scratching the chin. When a person is not being convinced by what someone is saying, the attention invariably wanders, and the eyes will stare away for an extended period. Use everything you've learned in this chapter in relation to disbelief, non-agreement and physical altercations.

Part 2: Physical Security Industry

This part of the book is going to cover two aspects of security. First, the industry as a whole. We're going to look at the fundamentals of physical security and identify numerous tools you can use to keep your company or client as safe as possible. Second, we're going to focus in on the world of casino security. The hope is that you'll be able to see the tools discussed in part one – being applied to the casino industry.

We chose the casino security arena because of how complex it is. What other industry is there where a security staff has to protect a resort, hotel, casino, and parking lot structure in addition to an insane amount of money? It's one heck of an undertaking.

There will be some overlap of topics being discussed (from part one). This is intentional. We hope your "security plan creativity" will be enhanced after reading part two of this book.

Chapter 4: Fundamentals Of Physical Security

Perception is strong and sight weak. In strategy it is important to see distant things as if they were close and to take a distanced view of close things.

~Miyamoto Musashi

Security Fundamentals & Concepts

It can be very easy for those of us working in standard detail assignments to slow our learning curve and just focus on our day in & day out responsibilities. But this is not for you! You want to be the type of professional that can articulate the concepts outlined below... on the spur of a moment. That spur of a moment may often be during a conversation with a potential employer when applying for a job.

I mean no disrespect, but a lot of the people I've worked with base their whole "Reason To Hire Me" on their distant past. Our past is very important and all of us bring a unique 'life-history' to this profession. However, in order to stay at in the top 10% of security professionals out there, we must combine our previous life-history with our current knowledge (and ability to articulate that...) along with impeccable customer service & a pleasant (not gung-ho) demeanor. Remember, when tooting your own horn... be able to tell the potential employer, "This is what I did years ago & this is what I'm doing today!"

Below are some concepts that you can use to enhance your understanding of the security profession. I know for some of you, it will be a review... which is always good for us!

Security Program "Musts"

When complete, our security or protection program must do these five things:

1. **Deter**... the bad guy from attempting to compromise our client.
2. **Detect**... any attempt of a compromise
3. **Delay**... the bad guys once they've begun their attack.
4. **Alert**... the Control Room & others as appropriate
5. **Respond**... the C.A.T (Counter Assault Team) and/or law enforcement.

The 7 Components of the Security Process

You may be asked to survey and develop the security program for your facility. The model below can assist you... when combined with good scheduling practices and a pre-planned annual calendar.

1.) Threat Assessment

2.) Risk Assessment

3.) Asset Determination

4.) Prevention - Develop Countermeasures

5.) Evaluate Countermeasures

6.) Develop Contingencies

7.) Evaluate Contingencies

* Cycle Back To #1

Rings Of Security

The three rings of security can be used for Residence or Facility security.

1. **Inner Ring**: Special Controlled Areas / Items
2. **Middle Ring**: Access To Facility; From Doors, Gates, Windows, to the property line fence or wall.
3. **Outer Ring**: From the Property line [Fences, Walls, (CPTED)] to One Mile Radius Around Your Property.

14 Security Tools

These 14 tools are helpful in reducing and eliminating security risks:

1. Armed / Unarmed Security
2. Coordination with Law Enforcement

3. Personnel with communications capability
4. Perimeter alarms
5. Personnel
6. Monitored alarms
7. Biometrics
8. Access control cards
9. Sophisticated locks
10. Security lighting
11. Barriers
12. Local alarms
13. Simple Locks
14. Specially Trained Dogs

Physical Security Ideas & Risks

In physical security, the term access control refers to the practice of restricting entrance to a property, a building, or a room to authorized persons. Physical access control can be achieved by a human (a guard, bouncer, or receptionist), through mechanical means such as locks and keys, or through technological means such as access control systems like the mantrap. Within these environments, physical key management may also be employed as a means of further managing and monitoring access to mechanically keyed areas or access to certain small assets.

Physical access control is a matter of who, where, and when. An access control system determines who is allowed to enter or exit, where they are allowed to exit or enter, and when they are allowed to enter or exit. Historically this was partially accomplished through keys and locks. When a door is locked only someone with a key can enter through the door depending on how the lock is configured. Mechanical locks and keys do not allow restriction of the key holder to specific times or dates. Mechanical locks and keys do not provide records of the key used on any specific door and the keys can be easily copied or transferred to an unauthorized person. When a mechanical key is lost or the key holder is no longer authorized to use the protected area, the locks must be re-keyed.

Electronic access control uses computers to solve the limitations of mechanical locks and keys. A wide range of credentials can be used to replace mechanical keys. The electronic access control system grants access based on the credential presented. When access is granted, the door is unlocked for a predetermined time and the transaction is recorded. When access is refused, the door remains locked and the attempted access is recorded. The system will also monitor the door and alarm if the door is forced open or held open too long after being unlocked.

Security Risks

The most common security risk of intrusion of an access control system is simply following a legitimate user through a door. Often the legitimate user will hold the door for the intruder. This risk can be minimized through security awareness training of the user population or more active means such as turnstiles. In very high security applications this risk is minimized by using a sally port, sometimes called a security vestibule or mantrap where operator intervention is required presumably to assure valid identification.

The second most common risk is from levering the door open. This is surprisingly simple and effective on most doors. The lever could be as small as a screwdriver or big as a crowbar. Fully implemented access control systems include forced door monitoring alarms. These vary in effectiveness usually failing from high false positive alarms, poor database configuration, or lack of active intrusion monitoring. Similar to levering, is crashing through cheap partition walls. In shared tenant spaces the divisional wall is a vulnerability. Along the same lines is breaking sidelights.

Spoofing locking hardware is fairly simple and more elegant than levering. A strong magnet can operate the solenoid controlling bolts in electric locking hardware. Motor locks, more prevalent in Europe than in the US, are also susceptible to this attack using a donut shaped magnet. It is also possible to manipulate the power to the lock either by removing or adding current.

Access cards themselves have proven vulnerable to sophisticated attacks. Enterprising hackers have built portable readers that capture the card number from a user's proximity card. The hacker simply walks by the user, reads the card, and then presents the number to a reader securing the door. This is possible when card numbers are sent in the clear, with no encryption being used.

Finally, most electric locking hardware still have mechanical keys as a fail-over. Mechanical key locks are vulnerable to bumping.

The Need-To-Know Principle

The 'need to know principle' can be enforced with user access controls and authorization procedures and its objective is to ensure that only authorized individuals gain access to information or systems necessary to undertake their duties.

Physical Security Fundamentals

Physical security describes security measures that are designed to deny unauthorized access to facilities, equipment and resources, and to protect personnel and property from damage or harm (such as espionage, theft, or terrorist attacks). Physical security involves the use of multiple layers of interdependent systems which include CCTV surveillance, security guards, protective barriers, locks, access control protocols, and many other techniques.

Physical security systems for protected facilities are generally intended to:

1. Deter potential intruders (e.g. warning signs and perimeter markings);
2. Detect intrusions and monitor/record intruders (e.g. intruder alarms and CCTV systems); and
3. Trigger appropriate incident responses (e.g. by security guards and police).

Ensure your security program / system addresses all the items on this "Rings of Security" graphic:

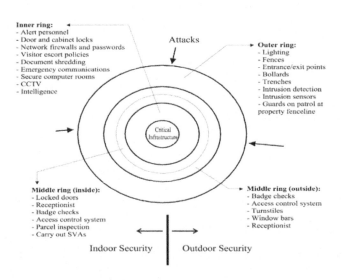

It is up to security designers, architects and analysts to balance security controls against risks, taking into account the costs of specifying, developing, testing, implementing, using, managing, monitoring and maintaining the controls, along with broader issues such as aesthetics, human rights, health and safety, and societal norms or conventions.

Physical access security measures that are appropriate for a high security prison or a military site may be inappropriate in an office, a home or a vehicle, although the principles are similar.

Elements and Design

Deterrence methods

The goal of deterrence methods is to convince potential attackers that a successful attack is unlikely due to strong defenses. The initial layer of security for a campus, building, office, or other physical space uses 'crime prevention through environmental design' aka CPTED, to deter threats. Some of the most common examples are also the most basic: warning signs or window stickers, fences, vehicle barriers, vehicle height-restrictors, restricted access points, security lighting and trenches.

Physical barriers

Spikes atop a barrier wall act as a deterrent to people trying to climb over the wall.

Physical barriers such as fences, walls, and vehicle barriers act as the outermost layer of security. They serve to prevent, or at least delay, attacks, and also act as a psychological deterrent by defining the perimeter of the facility and making intrusions seem more difficult. Tall fencing, topped with barbed wire, razor wire or metal spikes is often emplaced on the perimeter of a property, generally with some type of signage that warns people not to attempt to enter.

However, in some facilities imposing perimeter walls/fencing will not be possible (e.g. an urban office building that is directly adjacent to public sidewalks) or it may be aesthetically unacceptable (e.g. surrounding a shopping center with tall fences topped with razor wire); in this case, the outer security perimeter will be defined as the walls/windows/doors of the structure itself.

Natural surveillance (aka C.P.E.D.)

Another major form of deterrence that can be incorporated into the design of facilities is natural surveillance, whereby architects seek to build spaces that are more open and visible to security personnel and authorized users, so that intruders/attackers are unable to perform unauthorized activity without being seen. This is also known as "crime prevention through environmental design".

An example would be decreasing the amount of dense, tall vegetation in the landscaping so that attackers cannot conceal themselves within it, or placing critical resources in areas where intruders would have to cross over a wide, open space to reach them (making it likely that someone would notice them).

Security lighting

Security lighting is another effective form of deterrence. Intruders are less likely to enter well-lit areas for fear of being seen. Doors, gates, and other entrances should be well lit to allow close observation of people entering and exiting.

When lighting the grounds of a facility, widely-distributed low-intensity lighting is generally superior to small patches of high-intensity lighting, because the latter can have a tendency to create blind spots for security personnel and CCTV cameras. It is important to place lighting in a manner that makes it difficult to tamper with (e.g. suspending lights from tall poles), and to ensure that there is a backup power supply so that security lights will not go out if the electricity is cut off.

Intrusion detection and electronic surveillance

Alarm systems can be installed to alert security personnel when unauthorized access is attempted. Alarm systems work in tandem with physical barriers, mechanical systems, and security guards, serving to trigger a response when these other forms of security have been breached. They consist of sensors including motion sensors, contact sensors, and glass break detectors.

However, alarms are only useful if there is a prompt response when they are triggered. In the reconnaissance phase prior to an actual attack, some intruders will test the response time of security personnel to a deliberately tripped alarm system. By measuring the length of time it takes for a security team to arrive (if they arrive at all), the attacker can determine if an attack could succeed before authorities arrive to neutralize the threat. Loud audible alarms can also act as a psychological deterrent, by notifying intruders that their presence has been detected.

In some jurisdictions, law enforcement will not respond to alarms from intrusion detection systems unless the activation has been verified by an eyewitness or video. Policies like this one have been created to combat the 94–99 percent rate of false alarm activation in the United States.

Video surveillance

Surveillance cameras can be a deterrent when placed in highly visible locations and are also useful for incident verification and historical analysis. For example, if alarms are being generated and there is a camera in place, the camera could be viewed to verify the alarms. In instances when an attack has already occurred and a camera is in place at the point of attack, the recorded video can be reviewed.

Although the term closed-circuit television (CCTV) is common, it is quickly becoming outdated as more video systems lose the closed circuit for signal transmission and are instead transmitting on IP camera networks.

Video monitoring does not necessarily guarantee that a human response is made to an intrusion. A human must be monitoring the situation in real time in order to respond in a timely manner. Otherwise, video monitoring is simply a means to gather evidence to be analyzed at a later time. However, advances in information technology are reducing the amount of work required for video monitoring, through automated video analytics.

Access control

Access control methods are used to monitor and control traffic through specific access points and areas of the secure facility. This is done using a variety of systems including CCTV surveillance, identification cards, security guards, and electronic/mechanical control systems such as locks, doors, turnstiles and gates.

Mechanical access control systems

Mechanical access control systems include turnstiles, gates, doors, and locks. Key control of the locks becomes a problem with large user populations and any user turnover. Keys quickly become unmanageable, often forcing the adoption of electronic access control.

Electronic access control systems

Electronic access control manages large user populations, controlling for user lifecycles times, dates, and individual access points. For example, a user's access rights could allow access from 0700h to 1900h Monday through Friday and expires in 90 days.

These access control systems are often interfaced with turnstiles for Entry control in buildings to prevent unauthorized access. The use of turnstiles also reduces the need for additional security personnel to monitor each individual entering the building allowing faster throughput.

An additional sub-layer of mechanical/electronic access control protection is reached by integrating a key management system to manage the possession and usage of mechanical keys to locks or property within a building or campus.

Identification systems and access policies

Another form of access control (procedural) includes the use of policies, processes and procedures to manage the ingress into the restricted area. An example of this is the deployment of security personnel conducting checks for authorized entry at predetermined points of entry. This form of access control is usually supplemented by the earlier forms of access control (i.e. mechanical and electronic access control), or simple devices such as physical passes.

Security personnel

Security personnel play a central role in all layers of security. All of the technological systems that are employed to enhance physical security are useless without a security force that is trained in their use and maintenance, and which knows how to properly respond to breaches in security.

Security personnel perform many functions: as patrols and at checkpoints, to administer electronic access control, to respond to alarms, and to monitor and analyze video.

Physical Security Countermeasures

Consistent with effective security planning is the need to deploy appropriate risk reduction methods to minimize or eliminate identified vulnerabilities or mitigating consequences.

This section discusses many of the tools and countermeasures that should be considered in the implementation phase of planning as a means to improve the security of critical infrastructure and facilities, information systems, and other areas. Physical security countermeasures include these nine items:

1. Signs
2. Emergency telephones
3. Duress alarms, and assistance stations
4. Key controls and locks
5. Protective barriers
6. Protective lighting
7. Alarm and intrusion detection systems
8. Electronic access control systems
9. Surveillance systems and monitoring

What countermeasures to use in any given situation depends on what will be most useful, that is the utility of the countermeasure. Companies and agencies must examine the threats against the organization and identify the most useful means to reduce the vulnerabilities associated with those threats to acceptable levels. Utility is not solely a measure of cost. Often less costly, but more effective solutions are available that the agency can select to meet security requirements. In making these choices, security designers can benefit from the use of a utility scale that assimilates and compares one countermeasure against the other.

Countermeasures appear on the scale moving from "Less Protection, Less Cost and Less Effort to Greater Protection, Greater Cost, and Greater Effort." The figure does not provide relative comparisons of the three utility factors, but does provide them for each of the factors individually.

Once the utility of specific countermeasures has been evaluated, the company / agency should return to the concepts of systems approach, layered security, and systems integration when deciding how to proceed in reducing security vulnerabilities. Certain security design techniques or technologies are well suited to serve as "solution sets," capable of fulfilling security needs.

Signs

A rule of warfare that applies to homeland defense is that neither fences nor signs will deter or stop a determined enemy. However, security signs can play a very important role in the securing of facilities, rights-of-way, and critical infrastructure. Security signs are relatively inexpensive and low maintenance and can help deter aggressor actions or tactics.

Maintenance of a good security sign program also helps to create a working environment in which security is perceived to be taken seriously. Employees become aware of security requirements through well-placed signs that display the status of restricted or controlled areas or signs that limit or prohibit certain activities. The signs depicted in Figure 3-3 are approved by OSHA for use in the workplace. They represent a cross-section of security designs that cover both of these categories.

Attempt to do all of the following - From Least Cost, Effort, and Protection to Most Cost, Effort, and Protection:

1. Place trash receptacles as far away from the building as possible.

2. Remove any dense vegetation that may screen covert activity.

3. Use thorn-bearing plant materials to create natural barriers.

4. Identify all critical resources in the area (fire and police stations, hospitals, etc.).

5. Identify all potentially hazardous facilities in the area (nuclear plants, chemical labs, etc.).

6. Use temporary passive barriers to eliminate straight-line vehicular access to high-risk buildings.

7. Use vehicles as temporary physical barriers during elevated threat conditions.

8. Make proper use of signs for traffic control, building entry control, etc. Minimize signs identifying high-risk areas.

9. Identify, secure, and control access to all utility services to the building.

10. Limit and control access to all crawl spaces, utility tunnels, and other means of under building access to prevent the planting of explosives.

11. Utilize Geographic Information Systems (GIS) to assess adjacent land use.

12. Provide open space inside the fence along the perimeter.

13. Locate fuel storage tanks at least 100 feet from all buildings.

14. Block sight lines through building orientation, landscaping, screening, and landforms.

15. Use temporary and procedural measures to restrict parking and increase stand-off.

16. Locate and consolidate high-risk land uses in the interior of the site.

17. Select and design barriers based on threat levels.

18. Maintain as much stand-off distance as possible from potential vehicle bombs.

19. Separate redundant utility systems.

20. Conduct periodic water testing to detect waterborne contaminants.

21. Enclose the perimeter of the site. Create a single controlled entrance for vehicles (entry control point).

22. Establish law enforcement or security force presence.

23. Install quick connects for portable utility backup systems.

24. Install security lighting.

25. Install closed circuit television cameras.

26. Mount all equipment to resist forces in any direction.

27. Include security and protection measures in the calculation of land area requirements.

28. Design and construct parking to provide adequate stand-off for vehicle bombs.

29. Position buildings to permit occupants and security personnel to monitor the site.

30. Do not site the building adjacent to potential threats or hazards.

31. Locate critical building components away from the main entrance, vehicle circulation, parking, or maintenance area. Harden as appropriate.

32. Provide a site-wide public address system and emergency call boxes at readily identified locations.

33. Prohibit parking beneath or within a building.

34. Design and construct access points at an angle to oncoming streets.

35. Designate entry points for commercial and delivery vehicles away from high-risk areas.

36. In urban areas, push the perimeter out to the edge of the sidewalk by means of bollards, planters, and other obstacles. For better stand-off, push the line farther outward by restricting or eliminating parking along the curb, eliminating loading zones, or through street closings.

37. Provide intrusion detection sensors for all utility services to the building.

38. Provide redundant utility systems to support security, life safety, and rescue functions.

39. Conceal and/or harden incoming utility systems.

40. Install active vehicle crash barriers.

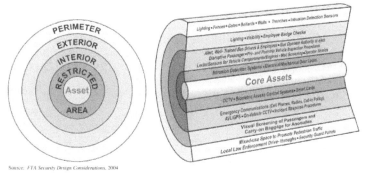

Source: *FTA Security Design Considerations*, 2004

Figure 3-2. Layers of security.

Source: http://www.safetysign.com

Figure 3-3. Security signs.

Effective use of signs starts with creation of a sign plan. This written record provides a framework for decision making about the installation, replacement, maintenance, and budgeting for the program. The sign plan identifies each sign by type and legend and contains a site plan for placement and installation.

In 2006, the U.S. Army Corps of Engineers updated its Sign Standards Manual EP 310-1-6a and EP 310-1-6b. The manual's Checklist of Sign Plan Elements shows the steps necessary to implement an effective sign plan.

The checklist includes 4 steps:

1. Inventory existing signs and their condition;

2. Collect or develop up-to-date pictorials, maps (optimally supported by GIS), diagrams, blueprints, or other representation of the area in need of protecting;

3. Prepare the site plan and sign layout materials; and

4. Implement the plan in conformance with established guidelines.

Once the implementation plan has been accomplished, a sign inspection and maintenance schedule should be developed. A budgeted coordinated sign replacement and maintenance schedule is necessary to reinforce the message to transportation system users, employees, and the public that the agency prioritizes security on its properties and facilities. Missing signs defeat the objectives of the security plan layout, while damaged or vandalized security signs reflect badly on the company / agency's commitment to security.

The Corps of Engineers recommends a formal inspection of security signs semi-annually. The inspection should identify signs requiring maintenance or replacement, signs that can be eliminated, and the need for additional signs. Vandalized, damaged, or missing signs should be repaired or replaced as quickly as possible.

Emergency Telephones, Duress Alarms & Assistance Stations

Historically, emergency alert or alarm systems have been hardwired communications systems linked to security control centers. Telephone boxes, panic alarm buttons, and intercom systems typically were linked to central stations where dispatchers or monitoring personnel answered emergency calls and sent response personnel to the location to help.

Today, wireless technology has added new dimensions and capabilities for the security-related use of these systems. For example, The State Transit Authority of Australia has a fleet of 1,800 buses in the Sydney and Newcastle area. Every bus is outfitted with Automatic Vehicle Locator (AVL) technology, a "Driver Duress Alarm," and a microphone that allows Authority central station personnel to hear what is happening on the vehicle when the driver activates the system.

Technology has also expanded the recipient group for duress alarms to include first responders themselves who can be equipped to receive a location-specific pre-recorded voice message using the officer's existing two-way radios. These systems by eliminating the monitoring station go-between can greatly improve the response time for police or security personnel in the event of a security incident. Information can be sent close to simultaneously to the command center by digital data packet transmittal.

Because of the high costs that can be associated with responding to duress alarms, companies and agencies should consider using emergency alert alarm systems to conduct a thorough risk assessment to correctly establish the size and scope of the project. Once the needs assessment has been completed, the best way to accomplish the countermeasures analysis is to engineer backwards from the response. Taking into account variables (e.g., time, distance, day of the week, and changes in staffing levels), police or security officer response capabilities, whether self-directed or through dispatch, should be examined to determine just how quickly help can arrive on the scene.

Next, prospective communications access points for deployment of emergency alert or alarm systems should be compared with estimated response capabilities, keeping in mind the potential time variation and, where applicable, the routes and locations of agency rolling stock. If additional security assets are required to make the system viable, they should be designed and planned for prior to implementation. A duress alarm or emergency communication system that often goes unanswered for an extended or unreasonable length of time creates an untenable security operating condition and should be avoided. Under such circumstances, alternative security countermeasures should be selected.

Key Control and Locks

It has been said that security starts and ends with closing the door and locking it. But the most expensive and well-built locking mechanism can be defeated if sufficient skill and enough time are available to the adversary or aggressor. According to the US Army Field Manual 19-30, Chapter 8, most key locks and conventional combination locks can be picked by an expert in a matter of minutes. More sophisticated manipulation-resistant locks, locks with four or more tumblers, some interchangeable core systems, or relocking devices on safes or doors can provide an appreciable increase in difficulty, but are still subject to compromise.

Locks should be considered at best to be a deterrent and more plausibly as a delay device that does not completely restrict entry to a protected area. Locks are a widely used basic security countermeasure for protecting facilities, activities, personnel, and property. They are present not only on doors, but on windows, gates, conveyances, interior offices, supply areas, filing cabinets, and virtually all kinds of other storage containers or areas as well.

Locking hardware is designed to various levels of deterrence or entry delay. Performance standards for locks based on these capabilities exist through ANSI/BHMAA Series 156 and United Laboratories (UL) 1034, 437, 768,294, 2058 and 305. It is recommended that the company consult with a professional locksmith for mechanical locks or security professional for electromechanical or electromagnetic locks before spending security funding on new hardware or upgrades.

Because keys and locks frequently are the only countermeasure used to protect assets and infrastructure, managing key access is fundamental to effective control. Maintaining a good key control system can mean the difference between having a robust security program and a compromised unsecure operating environment. The starting point for establishing an effective key control program is to develop a sound workable policy. The policy must be requirements-based and commensurate with the necessary levels of protection appropriate for the location or setting. Obtaining user input into the design of the key control system can help later when maintaining discipline associated with the system is important.

Management of the system should be assigned to an individual designated as the Key Control Officer (KCO). This individual should ensure the integrity of the key control process by doing these 6 things:

1. Exercising approval authority over the acquisition and storage of all locks and keys,
2. Overseeing the distribution of keys to agency employees,
3. Conducting inspections and inventories,
4. Maintaining the organization's key depository,
5. Investigating key loss, and
6. Establishing an official records maintenance system that serves as the control point for all agency key and lock activity.

Frequently, an organization will face a situation in which key control has been compromised, either through a lack of attention to security or by the failure of one or more employees to comply with policy. When current conditions demand the system and process be revised, the agency should create a key control annex to their physical security plan. The newly assigned KCO should conduct a comprehensive survey of all agency physical assets needing protection to establish a baseline key control plan that can return efficiency to the program. Under this program, when a compromised key access point is identified, locks should be replaced, recoded, or otherwise upgraded as a security plan priority.

Protective Barriers

Protective barriers include fencing, other types of barriers, and landscape design. Each of these three categories will be discussed.

Fencing

The two main issues with the use of fencing as a protective barrier are:

1. Placement and
2. The grade or strength of fencing material.

Substituting other types of protective barriers where fencing traditionally has been used should be considered. The agency should look at the design aspects of both placement and strength of materiel in concert to determine how the use of fencing countermeasures can reduce risk.

Placement

The chief use of fencing for security is as a deterrent or delaying factor. When fencing is used this way, terms such as perimeter line and controlled access zone apply. The perimeter line is the outermost line of defense for an area being protected. A controlled access zone attempts to limit access to the more immediate area being protected.

The uses of fencing in these configurations are clear. For example, a fence can be used to form the outermost perimeter line. Fencing (or more generally protective barriers) used in conjunction with layered defense principles offers a much broader range of security applications. FEMA 430, Site and Urban Design for Security presents a three-layer model for protecting a building against attack. Under this approach, the objective is to "create a defense in depth by creating cumulative successive obstacles that must be penetrated . . . penetration of the perimeter leads only to further defense systems that must be overcome."

Figure 3-4 illustrates the use of fencing as a security countermeasure in conjunction with the first and second defensive layers. In this configuration, the greater the distance between the building exterior and the perimeter line, the better. This "open space" concept of security permits designers to use an array of different security countermeasures to defend the organization's assets, including line of sight observation, video surveillance, motion detection, and other intrusion detection technologies.

Strength of Material

Security planners can use fencing to prevent as well as deter. Depending on the deployment and K Certification class of fencing material, certain aggressor tactics can be completely defeated.

Primarily, threats that can be prevented relate to explosives mitigation and involve barrier related interception of the threat at a point that creates sufficient stand-off distance to absorb dangerous explosive blast levels. K Certification anti-ram standards originated at the Department of State. The rating is determined from perpendicular barrier impact results of a truck weighing 15,000 lb (6810 kg) striking the barrier straight on. To meet the standard, the truck's cargo bed cannot penetrate the barrier by more than 1 meter. Figure 3-5 provides additional information about the vehicle and crash ratings associated with the truck striking the barriers at speeds of 30, 40, and 50 mph. Figure 3-6 shows a crash-rated fence that, according to the manufacturer, can be reinforced with an integrated cable system to meet K8 standards. Figure 3-7 shows a cable barrier that can be used for fencing reinforcement.

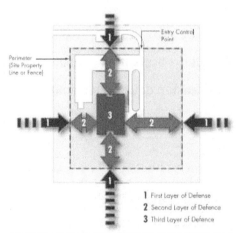

1 First Layer of Defense
2 Second Layer of Defence
3 Third Layer of Defence

Source: FEMA 430, *Building, Site and Layout Design Guidance to Mitigate Potential Terrorist Attacks*, 2007

Figure 3-4. *Use of fencing as a security countermeasure with defensive layers.*

Certification Class	Speed (mph)	Speed (kph)
K12	50	80
K8	40	65
K4	30	48

(a)

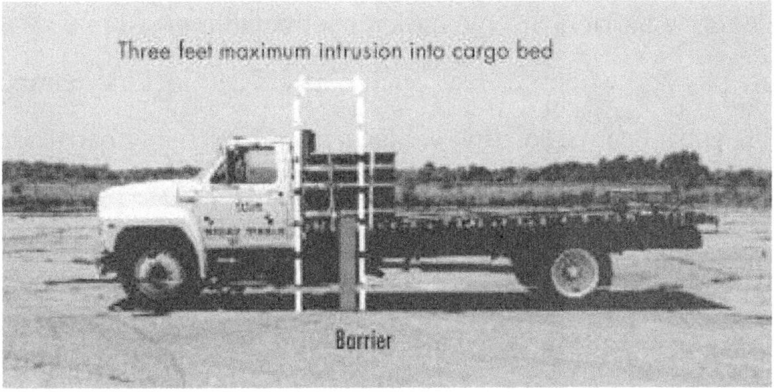

(b)

Figure 3-5. Vehicle and crash ratings (a) and truck striking barrier (b).

Fences are only one type of protective barrier available to security designers. Other types of barriers include anti-ram vehicle barriers categorized as either passive or active. Anti-ram barrier effectiveness is based on a formula:

$$KE = \frac{Mv^2}{2}$$

Source: FEMA 426, *Building Design for Homeland Security*, 2004

Where M is the mass of the vehicle and v is the velocity at the time of impact. Passive barriers are fixed countermeasures and include bollards (concrete-filled steel pipe), reinforced street furniture, concrete walls, planters, and berms (see Figure 3-8).

Active barriers are movable or retractable in some way so as to allow passage when needed. Such barriers can include retractable bollards, crash beams, rotating wedge systems, or rising barricades as shown in Figures 3-9 through 3-11.

Landscape Design

Natural barriers, such as trees or water, can be used to reduce vulnerabilities. In addition, actual site planning for protected areas can be security minded with landscape design serving the dual purposes of aesthetics and function (see Figure 3-12).

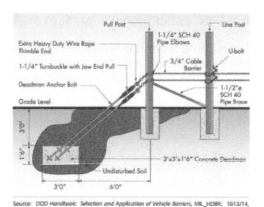

Source: DOD Handbook: Selection and Application of Vehicle Barriers, MIL_HDBK: 1013/14, 1999

Figure 3-7. Cable barrier deployable as a means for fencing reinforcement.

Protective Lighting

Security professionals, emergency response personnel, and safety practitioners extol the value of manufactured light to protect people and property from harm or unreasonable risk of injury.

Used as a security countermeasure during hours of darkness, protective lighting can create an operating environment that provides better security than in the daytime. This can occur when security designers use capabilities such as glare projection to reduce the ability of an adversary to see inside a protected area. Protective lighting objectives include the following:

Adherence to acceptable industry standards for outdoor protective lighting levels as promulgated by the Illuminated Engineering Society of North America (IESNA) or the guidelines of the New Buildings Institute's Advanced Lighting Guidelines, 2003 Edition:

1. Illumination of all exterior points within the perimeter of the protected area, including walkways, vehicle entranceways, fence lines, and critical structures or assets;
2. Non-transgressing illumination of approach areas to the perimeter line;
3. Deterrence of aggressor attempts at entry to protected areas;

4. Support for other security countermeasures (e.g., video surveillance cameras, motion-activated sensors, or security forces); and
5. Resistance to tampering, vandalism, neutralization, or defeat.

Top: Combination of low retaining walls and low bollards. Bottom, left: Combination of oversize bollard and large planters placed on very wide sidewalk. Bottom, right: Combination of tree and bollards.

Source: FEMA 430, *Building, Site and Layout Design Guidance to Mitigate Potential Terrorist Attacks*, 2007

Figure 3-8.   Barriers as countermeasures.

Source: FEMA 430, *Building, Site and Layout Design Guidance to Mitigate Potential Terrorist Attacks*, 2007

Figure 3-9.   Examples of retractable bollards and crash beams.

Source: FEMA 430, *Building, Site and Layout Design Guidance to Mitigate Potential Terrorist Attacks*, 2007

Figure 3-10.   Mobile wedge barrier.

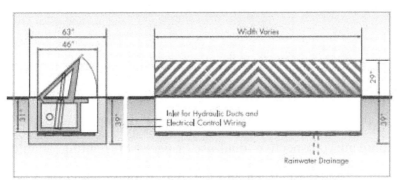

Source: FEMA 430, *Building, Site and Layout Design Guidance to Mitigate Potential Terrorist Attacks*, 2007

Figure 3-11.   Rising barricade.

This proposal for the re-design of the Washington Monument grounds uses water to create a barrier. The meandering canal is beautiful as well as functional.

Source: Michael Van Vandenburgh and Associates

Figure 3-12. Proposal for the re-design of the Washington Monument grounds.

As with other measures, protective lighting security planning requires thoughtful and careful study to make the most of the benefits of the program. In particular, because of the open access of the environment, prospective dual-use aspects of lighting should be examined for potential integration into mainstream transportation operations. Similarly, the security applicability of lighting configurations should be factored into operational planning and decision making.

Planners should also determine the upgrade prospects of the existing lighting system. Taking advantage of opportunities to retrofit existing lighting systems (luminaries) can improve lighting quality, reduce electricity use, and extend time between required maintenance and replacement, while providing benefits such as improved security or safety.

In this regard, although relatively inexpensive when compared with other security strategies, lighting plans also require a strong continuing commitment to maintenance and upkeep.

Table 3-1. Lamp types.

Type	Life (in hrs)	Efficiency*	Advantages**	Disadvantages**
Incandescent	500 – 4000	17 – 22	Inexpensive	Relatively short life
Fluorescent	9,000 – 17,000	67 – 100	Longer life than incandescent and metal halide	Shorter life than mercury vapor and HPS
HID Mercury Vapor Metal Halide HPS	24,000+ 6,000 24,000	31 – 63 80 – 115 80 – 140	Longest life. Good efficiency More efficient than mercury vapor Long life and excellent efficiency	May not be optimal in conditions where full illumination is required immediately on activation. Depending on the type of lamp—mercury vapor, metal halide, or high-pressure sodium (HPS), the time required for HID lamps to reach full light output can range from 3 to 7 minutes. Re-strike times (cooling time required before the lamp will re-start) can be even longer—ranging from 3 to 15 minutes.

* in lumens per watt
** compared with other lamps
(Source: Adapted from NFPA 730 Guide for Premises Security, 2006)

Agencies must budget for scheduled cleaning and replacement of luminaries. Different types of lighting systems can reduce the overall costs associated with upkeep while improving the efficiency of the lighting output, measured luminance (foot candles or lux).

Lamps

Three principal sources of light are in common use:

1. Incandescent lamps,
2. Fluorescent lamps and,
3. High-intensity discharge (HID) lamps.

All three types convert electrical energy to light or radiant energy.

Luminaries

Luminaries (consisting of a complete lighting unit, lamp, housing, and power supply connectivity) are categorized as follows:

1. Floodlights,
2. Streetlights,
3. Fresnel lenses, and
4. Searchlights.

Table 3-2 provides a comparison of these categories.

Table 3-2. Comparison of lights.

Type	Purposes	Description	Lamps Used
Floodlight	To project to distant points. To illuminate perimeter fence lines, critical facilities, and high-priority assets	Designed with a focused beam width that can be projected to distant points, thereby illuminating a specified area or location. Use in homeland defense is vital. Used to illuminate perimeter fence lines, boundaries, critical facilities, and high-priority assets.	Incandescent HID
Streetlight	To illuminate large areas and entranceways.	Used to illuminate large areas. Their light distribution patterns can be either symmetrical or asymmetrical. Symmetrical street light luminaries are placed in locations that will cascade light throughout the area to be covered. Asymmetrical street lights direct light by reflection or refraction into the area to be lighted. Mercury vapor lamps are widely used in street lighting because of their long life.	Mercury vapor
Fresnel lens	To protect high-security locations where transgressing light will not affect the neighboring community	Directional high-glare units that project a fan-shaped light beam approximately 180 degrees in the horizontal and 15 to 30 degrees in the vertical	Incandescent HID
Searchlight	To augment fixed lighting at a given location	Provides a powerful concentrated beam. Ranges from 12 to 24 inches in diameter of reflection and from 250 to 3,000 watts. Often portable	Incandescent

Alarm and Intrusion Detection Systems

Alarms can detect various types of incidents (e.g., intrusion, smoke or fire, temperature change, gas, or water flow rates), as well as other emergency conditions. Their basic physical security application, however, relates principally to intrusion detection. The functionality also applies to chemical, biological, and radiological sensors, although they are more complex depending on the technology associated with the types of sensors.

Intrusion detection alarm systems are an important countermeasure in the security planning toolkit. Their main purpose is to work as a force multiplier to allow for more efficient use of staffing by reducing the number of security personnel required to patrol or monitor a protected area. Assuming that a response force is nearby, alarm systems can eliminate the need for a dedicated security patrol force.

Alarm systems can be used:

- o In place of other security countermeasures that are not viable because of safety concerns or operational requirements or
- o As a supplemental security measure.

The 4 main elements of an intrusion detection alarm system are the:

1. Sensors
2. The alarm processor
3. The monitoring system
4. The communications architecture that connects these elements

The 7 components of an alarm system include the following:

1. Main Control Unit
2. Keypad
3. Input Devices (Sensors)
4. Transformer
5. Power Supply
6. Telecommunications, and
7. Output Devices

An alarm system can be hard wired (the system uses wires to connect all input and output devices to the main control unit) or wireless (the system uses radio waves or RF to transmit intrusion alarms). Some systems, known as hybrids, use a combination of both hard-wired and wireless signal carrying methods to communicate intrusion or status.

The physical security deployment of intrusion detection systems usually occurs with other security counter measures such as natural and manmade barriers, access control systems, and other sensor technologies. For an intrusion detection alarm system to be effective, there must be both an active or passive monitoring capability and a security or law enforcement personnel response team capacity.

Sensors are the input devices for intrusion detection systems. Interior sensors detect intruders:

1. Approaching or penetrating a secured boundary (e.g., a door, wall, roof, floor, vent, or window);
2. Moving within a secured area (e.g., a room or hallway); and
3. Moving, lifting, or touching a particular object.

Exterior sensors detect intruders crossing a perimeter or boundary or entering a protected zone. Although many interior sensors should not be exposed to weather, exterior sensors must be able to withstand outdoor weather conditions. Exterior sensors have a higher nuisance alarm rate than their interior counterparts and a lower probability of detection, primarily because of uncontrollable environmental factors.

Many different types of sensors are used in intrusion detection alarm systems. These sensors detect through sound, vibration, motion, and electrostatic and/or light beams. Determining which sensors to deploy in response to security vulnerability depends on both operational considerations (e.g., the facility's hours of operation; the presence of system users, staff, or other personnel; the value of material, equipment, or other critical assets; and the response time of security forces) and technological limitations (e.g., concerns about radio and electrical interference, sound levels, weather and climate, and other environmental factors). Ideally, the agency should seek professional security assistance in planning for intrusion detection alarm systems.

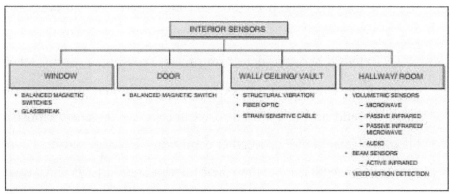

Source: SAVER Summary, Handbook of Intrusion Detection Sensors, 2004 http://www.dhs-saver.info

Figure 3-14. *Interior intrusion sensors—applications index.*

Electronic Access Control Systems

Access control systems limit or restrict the access of personnel or vehicles either into or out of a controlled zone or area. The technology used can be basic or complicated, depending on the needs and requirements of the resource or area to be protected. Systems can stand alone to control access to a single-entry point or be multi-portal, computer-based, and capable of controlling access to hundreds of doors and managing thousands of identification credentials.

Before implementing an access control system, the agency should have a well-defined understanding of the threats and vulnerabilities to be addressed. In addition, sensitivity to the following 8 factors is important:

1. The nature and tempo of activity in and around the protected area;
2. The size of the authorized population;
3. Variation in degrees of accessibility in terms of access levels and time;
4. The physical characteristics of the area being protected;
5. Limitations or restrictions caused by the operating environment;
6. Climate and weather conditions affecting system operations;
7. Staffing, training, and support levels available for operating and maintaining the system; and

8. The availability of security forces to respond to a report of an unauthorized entry.

Protecting company operations and assets can be a difficult proposition. Because of the open and ubiquitous operating environment, it is not always possible to control people's movements. Inappropriate screening of system users may create an untenable level of inconvenience that results in the loss of customers. Similarly, an agency whose employees are confronted with unnecessary, time-consuming access control regimens will, at best, suffer a loss of productivity through queuing or, at worst, have the system itself compromised by activities such as door propping.

Access control performance must correspond to the needs of the organization by being responsive to throughput requirements, defined as "the measure of the number of authorized persons or vehicles that can process through an ingress or egress point within a period of time." (SAVER Summary; Handbook of Intrusion Detection Sensors, 2004)

The accurate identification of controlled or restricted areas through a rigorous determination of what locations, assets, or resources need protection is essential to achieving acceptable throughput. The difference between the two is based on the necessity of access. Controlled area access should be limited to persons who have official business within the area. Restricted area admittance should be limited to personnel assigned to work in the particular area or other personnel who have been expressly cleared and authorized.

Other individuals entering restricted areas should be accompanied at all times by an authorized individual. The following 6 criteria can assist in defining agency-controlled areas or restricted areas:

1. Operating areas critical to continued operation or provision of services
2. Locations where uncontrolled access would interfere or disrupt personnel in the performance of their duties
3. Storage areas that contain valuable equipment or materials
4. Locations where operations can result in the existence of hazardous or unsafe conditions
5. Office areas where sensitive or confidential information is located, and
6. Command and control areas that house critical functions

The 4 main elements of an access control system are:

1. Barriers
2. Verification or identification equipment
3. Panels, and

4. The communications structure that connects these elements

Source: SAVER Summary; Handbook of Intrusion Detection Sensors, 2004 http://www.dhs-saver.info
Figure 3-15. Cipher access control barrier.

The system must also be able to communicate either directly or indirectly through human interface with response security forces.

Access control barriers are identification-based, requiring the person or vehicle requesting access to possess some form of information or technology that can be read by the system. Electronic systems are computer-controlled with access determinations made through the query of an authorized user database.

Figure 3-15 shows a cipher access control barrier widely used in areas that require frequent entry by authorized users. The cipher lock controls access using information the individual knows (a combination).

Figure 3-16 shows a token-based drop arm barrier system used to supplement security personnel at the vehicle entranceway to a controlled area. The vehicle contains some form of a readable proximity sticker, such as a bar code or other device that automatically lifts the drop arm barrier once the authorized user database has been interrogated.

Source: SAVER Summary; *Handbook of Intrusion Detection Sensors*, 2004 http://www.dhs-saver.info

Figure 3-16. Token-based drop arm barrier system.

There are many types of access control system barriers and perhaps even more identification methods - there are at least nine different card-encoding technologies available, including the better-known technologies such as magnetic stripe or proximity.

Today smartcard technology and biometric systems are becoming more and more prevalent. Smart card technology is used to describe a single card that performs more than one function (e.g., access control and photographic identification).

Access control-related biometric technology differs from cipher in that the individual seeking entry knows authorizing information and a token, based on something the individual possesses, is read by the barrier. As shown in Figure 3-17, biometric technology is based on who the individual is.

TCRP Report 86, Volume 4: Intrusion Detection for Public Transportation Facilities Handbook contains a checklist for sizing or engineering an access control system (see Table 3-3). However, this list should only be used in conjunction with the help of security professionals specializing in designing and implementing access control systems. Establishing an integrated access control system can be complex, given that the effort involves both short- and long-term issues of design, maintenance, continued operation, training, and testing.

Access control systems can be expensive and costs are easy to underestimate. Expenditures associated with system infrastructure can climb quickly as the organization's needs grow and mature. Security planners should contemplate access control implementation based on lifecycle costs and multi-year capital planning.

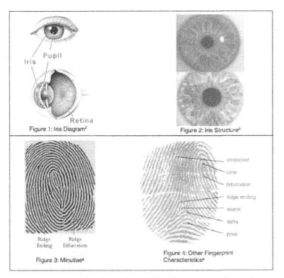

Figure 3-17. Biometric technologies including iris recognition, fingerprint identification, voice recognition and palm print identification.

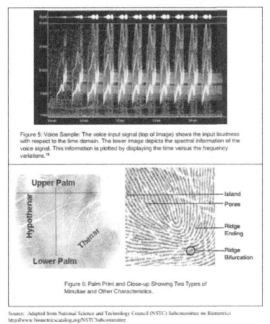

Source: Adapted from National Science and Technology Council (NSTC) Subcommittee on Biometrics http://www.biometricscatalog.org/NSTCSubcommittee

Figure 3-17. Continued.

Surveillance Systems and Monitoring

More and more every day CCTV is being used as a security countermeasure for both homeland security and crime prevention. The public has, for the most part, accepted the presence of video cameras in public places as a routine part of their daily coming and goings. Video systems can now be observed in use in facilities such as banks, shopping centers, transportation facilities, casinos, gas stations, convenience stores, and stadiums. Outdoor surveillance cameras are being mounted in downtown districts in major cities, highways, parks and recreation areas, and even at intersections where traffic violators are being caught on film running red lights.

Table 3-3. Checklist for sizing or engineering an access control system.

Order	System Characteristic	Explanation	Information Needed
1	Number of Locations	Is this system for one physical location or multiple locations?	List of locations
2	Network Connectivity	If multiple locations, what kind of network connectivity exists between the sites?	Example T-1 data line, or via Internet
3	Area of Containment	Is area enclosed by security barriers? Fences, Walls, Building, Gates/Portals	Area map with barriers and gates identified for each location
4	System Zones	How many security zones? These are areas of limited access (by time, training, need, etc.)	Defined zones on map
5	Access Rules	Need to determine rules for access to systems zones. A matrix of personnel and business/safety rules that allow access. Example = Chief of Security has full access all the time. Office janitor has access to public administration building during work hours only.	Full list in matrix form
6	Gates/Doors/Portal	What are the number of personnel and vehicle portals? (Portal = gate, door, etc.)	A count of portals by type
7	Personnel Tracking	Is there a need to know if people are either in or out? Or just secure check in is needed? Secure in & out requires ACS readers on both sides of gate / portal	Secure in & out or just secure in—by location
8	Material Tracking	Is there a need to track vehicles, trucks, computers or other 'materials'?	Yes or no. If yes provide a list.
9	Number of Badges	How many people = number of badges. (Badges = Access Cards)	Count
10	Number of Trackers	If tracking materials is needed, how many?	Count by type
11	Hazardous Conditions	Area card reader installed in hazardous locations?	Limits types of readers
12	Biometrics	Are biometrics used, and if so what type?	Yes or no. If yes what type?
13	Reader Type	What type of reader? Examples = RF proximity, Biometric	Reader Type
14	Badge Type	What type of badge is needed?	Follow Reader Type
15	Badge Information	What information is needed on badge? Name, photo, employee number, etc.	Graphic of front & back of badge with ALL data
16	Badge Production	Need to determine number & type of badging stations. Input included number, type, and physical locations	Count & location of badging production stations.
17	Tracker Information	What information is needed on the material tracker 'badge'?	Full description
18	Traffic	How many people use the system on a daily basis?	Number of accesses. In & Out = 2

19	History	How much data is to be saved, including badges issued, portals transferred, access changes, period of data retention.	Study of traffic to size ACS data storage requirements
20	Data Integration	Does the ACS interface with other systems? Examples include HR, time & attendance, etc.	Data integration plan with database mapping
21	Intrusion Detection	Is an IDS present? If so what type of integration is required?	Yes or no. If yes list interfaces
22	Video Interface	Is there an interface between ACS and video systems?	Video at portals? Badge photo pop up upon access?
23	Computer OS	Is there a preferred Computer Operating System?	Influence on chosen ACS
24	Installation Support	Is support labor for installation readily available?	In house, contract, turnkey?
25	System Support	Is support labor for maintenance & repair available?	In house or outsource?
26	System Operation	Is support labor available for system operation?	In house or outsource?

Source: *TCRP Report 86, Volume 4 Intrusion Detection for Public Transportation Facilities Handbook*

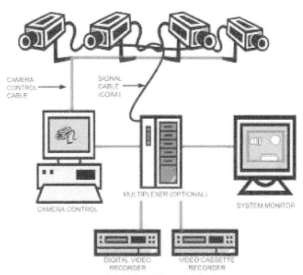

Source: SAVER Highlight, CCTV Technology, 2005 http://www.dhs-saver.info

Figure 3-18. SAVER highlight CCTV.

The term CCTV is synonymous with surveillance technology and has come to be used as a generic descriptor for video systems. Originally the term was used to differentiate between broadcast television and private video networks. In general, CCTV is a system of one or more video cameras connected in a closed circuit or loop. The cameras provide input images to a television monitor for viewing. Depending on security objectives, the CCTV system may also include a recording and playback capability (see Figure 3-18).

Effectively integrating CCTV into a transportation agency's security program demands that planners exercise a high level of conceptual understanding of the capabilities of the technology and its ability to meet organizational requirements and needs. Video systems do not provide any form of denial of attack or delay in response to aggressor tactics or actions. They present no physical barrier, nor do they control access or reduce exposure to dangerous conditions. In the strictest sense, CCTV seeks to deter aggressor actions or targeting through an increase in the aggressor's perceived risk of capture or his belief in the successful interdiction and prevention of an attack. Recognition of this circumstance means that to effectively deploy CCTV as a deterrent requires aggressor knowledge of the presence of the system. In addition, the aggressor must believe that the CCTV system will indeed prevent or reduce the likelihood of success (see Figure 3-19).

With an overt CCTV camera, the public (and offenders) can clearly see the surveillance camera and determine the direction in which it is facing.
Source: US DOJ, *Video Surveillance of Public Places* by Jerry Ratcliffe, 2006

Figure 3-19. Overt CCTV camera.

CCTV also serves a second almost equally important role as a security tool capable of greatly improving the performance and responsiveness of security forces and intrusion detection systems, including alarm and access control.

By adding video surveillance to these systems, an agency can remotely monitor and assess security conditions during a security incident. In fact, currently available advanced video surveillance technologies can further expand the effectiveness of video monitoring. Switchers that permit operators to select between video images, multiplexers that facilitate simultaneous viewing, and new video analytic capabilities are in use to aid operators by directing their attention to priority images (see Figure 3-20).

Technology such as facial recognition software and thermal imaging systems can further increase the value of video surveillance (see Figure 3-21).

In 2007, the American Public Transportation Association (APTA) published The Selection of Cameras, Digital Recording Systems, Digital High Speed Train-lines and Networks for use in Transit related CCTV Systems, as a part of its IT Standards Program Recommended Practice (RP) Series. APTA IT-RP-001-07 V1.2 is a valuable technical resource for Companies and agencies considering implementation or upgrading of CCTV systems. The document covers the selection and use of cameras for CCTV at stations as well as on moving transportation conveyances such as buses or train cars. Recording devices and backbone architecture for support of CCTV are discussed in detail. In its overview section the APTA RP states:

This level of quality is intended to facilitate the requirements of the systems design through a formal 'Systems Requirement Specification' (SRS) allowing the systems to be designed for every day safety and security requirements as well as revenue protection and anti-crime and anti-terrorist applications requiring the identification of unknown people and objects depicted within images and allow systems to be designed to meet the 4 industry accepted categories known as Detect, Monitor, Identify and Recognize.

The industry-accepted categories of *Detect, Monitor, Identify, and Recognize* are used by APTA to frame the functional requirements of CCTV systems. Specifications are based on image resolution criteria that depend on the security purpose and use for the video system. Figure 3-22 provides a comparison of screen size image projections for these categories.

This semi-covert CCTV camera may have a crime prevention advantage over an overt system because offenders can never be sure in which direction that camera is facing.

Source: US DOJ, *Video Surveillance of Public Places* by Jerry Ratcliffe, 2006

Figure 3-20.   Overt CCTV camera.

Figure 3-21. Thermal imaging camera (a) and photo (b).

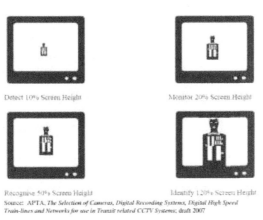

Figure 3-22. Screen size image projections.

The photographic images in the bottom two pictures are cropped, enlarged, and enhanced from the photos immediately above them.

The determination of image resolution requirements is perhaps the most important aspect of CCTV system design. Without usable images, security personnel cannot discharge their responsibilities. However, the costs attributable to CCTV design can increase exponentially when security planners overreach the system capabilities to meet criteria that serve no objective purpose.

This problem extends not just to image quality but also to the functionality of the other component parts of video systems. CCTV design should start with a needs and requirements analysis based on the findings of the agency's risk assessment. Activity-driven performance functions should be identified that articulate each vulnerability or security objective that the CCTV system should address.

I hope I've provided a nice overview of physical security for you. Additionally, I hope by mentioning the sources of information, you'll be inclined to study the topic further. If you're ever in need of a quick brush-up on any of these topics or you need a specific security plan – use the internet! Here are some sample searches:

(Google)	disaster recovery plan pdf
(Google)	security survey pdf
(YouTube)	security lighting 101 basics
(YouTube)	access control systems 101 basics

Chapter 5: Casino Security

I think we're going to the moon because it's in the nature of the human being to face challenges. It's by the nature of his deep inner soul... we're required to do these things just as salmon swim upstream.

~Neil Armstrong

Introduction to Casino Security

Casinos need to focus on an outside – in approach. We start from the property line. Then we move in and thru the parking lots. Next is the exterior of the buildings. Finally, we're inside the casino and looking at interior access controls, cash rooms, vaults, fire routes and more. For the property line & exterior of the building, good CPTED must be used. This stands for Crime Prevention Through Environmental Design.

The Property Line

Fences, block walls, tree lines and signage can be used here. The goal is to separate the casino from neighboring properties and to control incoming & outgoing traffic. (foot and vehicle). What we can't physically control – we observe & record! For this to work, lighting should be excellent.

The Exterior Of The Building(s)

There are six sides to every building. The roof, floor (accessed via basements and sub levels) and the walls. Penetrating these areas should be very difficult. All sides have weaknesses that must be strengthened. Knowing routines of staff, deliveries, etc. will give bad guys an advantage when it comes to gaining access. Extra attention must be given to unusual points of entry such as doors, windows, delivery docks and skylights.

Interior Access Control

From access control ropes, tapes and signs… to locks on doors and cabinets… to high dollar access control systems which include motion sensors, glass breaks, etc.

Barriers, while very basic, serve two basic areas in security. Physical & psychological. Both areas can deter and/or delay criminal activity. Barriers are used as soon as you enter a casino property – such as parking lot controls. They're also used inside to 'steer' foot traffic, control line movement, etc.

Casino Surveillance

Most casinos have two common positions in the security department. The security officer and the surveillance officer. The surveillance officer tends to be behind the scenes and in a lot of cases, is a harder job to obtain. The reasoning is the knowledge base needed to run the CCTV systems, understanding the games being played and the ability to read body language and intent.

I've seen casino surveillance officers who were **incredibly talented**. They are probably the most underestimated folks in private security. What will you be looking for if assigned as a surveillance officer? Let's start with the obvious… gaming thieves! People try to steal from casinos all day long…. every day. People used to attach tape or string to coins / tokens and try to steal from slot machines (although card systems are being used more and more). Others will create multi-thief scams and try to outsmart the casino by taking advantage of perceived weaknesses in dealers, routines, etc.

Assaults, robbery, rape and other crimes are also on the mind of a professional surveillance officer. There is a **huge** quantity of people that pass through a casino on a daily basis. This makes it impossible for the officers on the floor to see everything that's going on.

The surveillance officer and the quality CCTV system can be the eyes (and ears in some cases) for the floor officer.

Con Games & Scams

As mentioned before, players often times will try to cheat the casino out of money. This is one reason why understanding the games on the floor is so important by members of the security staff.

In addition to player cons… a casino also has to worry about internal theft and scams. Bad employees come with the industry so they must be watched also. Stealing chips to getting involved in scam rings has gotten many employees fired and/or arrested.

Don't forget about the old tricks like fake "slip n falls" by players and/or employees. Casinos must protect themselves against fraudulent insurance and or workers comp cases too.

The casino security industry is incredibly complex. Regardless of the country you live, you can be sure that many federal, state, province, local and/or tribal laws will affect the daily business of casinos. Know the laws of your area.

Physical Security

Role of The Security Officer

On a basic level, the security officer is employed to protect the property, personnel, guests, money & information of the casino.

However, due to the complexity of the environment, the intelligence of the bad guys, the number of casinos players can choose to go to and the legalities of the industry – a security officer today has a much larger role.

One role a security officer has is to enhance or at a minimum - compliment – the professionalism & image of the casino. There are two key things to address when we discuss a security officer complimenting the image of the casino. First there are the uniforms and second are the officers themselves.

The Uniform

The uniform needs to do these four things.

1. It needs to announce the person wearing it as casino security.
2. It needs to look respectful and be in the image of the casino management
3. It needs to make the employee wearing it feel good about being in it and representing the casino.
4. It needs to have as much an authoritative effect on patrons as possible.

Knowing the above should make it completely clear that a rent-a-cop uniform, with epilates and a badge is NOT acceptable.

Looking at the requirements above – let's break this old school uniform down on a Pass – Fail scale:

1. Pass - It needs to announce the person wearing it as casino security.
    a. People know who they are right away.
2. Fail - It needs to look respectful and be in the image of the casino management
    a. It's not respectful. As a matter of fact, the uniform shouts minimum wage employee.
3. Fail - It needs to make the employee wearing it feel good about being in it and representing the casino.
    a. The first thing an employee wearing this uniform wants to do if someone they know walks in – **is hide**.
4. Fail - It needs to have as much an authoritative effect on patrons as possible.
    a. Patrons who see this uniform walk up get their insults ready asap. Wanna-be, rent-a-cop, high school dropout, etc. "Go get me someone who's really in charge." "What? Just got out of the military and can't get a real job?" "Rejected from the policy academy, eh?"

All of these "fails" can be prevented when you have a physically fit officer wearing a professional blazer, slacks & ear piece.

Male or female doesn't matter. Physical fitness, calmness, respectable uniform and the ability to let verbal insults slide, is what counts.

The Officers

Deterring Crimes & Unauthorized Activity

A professional security officer who remains visible will deter most crime and unwanted behaviors. Notice I said 'most' and not 'all'. Let's be honest, a lot of bad guys are very intelligent with the methods they use. They will often 'test' a casino by behaving in somewhat suspicious manners, just to observe the response. (if any)

The proof that visible security officers are a deterrent can be shown in statements made by criminals. Often times they've stated that the reason they chose Casino A over Casino B (to steal from or choose assault victims) is because they were uncomfortable with the security presence in Casino B.

Here's an interesting fact. Many officers will patrol... prevent a crime just by their visibility... and not even know it. It's not until a CCTV audit that instances like this are noticed.

Reality Check

Will patrols eliminate all crimes? No – but they sure do minimize most attempts. Criminals prefer to hit the easier targets, whether their target is a person or a place. DON'T be the easiest target. Create an environment that is so active with security presence that bad guys prefer to move on to a softer target.

Improving Public Relations

Greetings

Looking guests & players in the eye, saying hello, good afternoon, good evening or good morning (with a smile) and holding doors should be common. Unfortunately, it's not. Doing these things shows confidence, class and attentiveness. Those three things help build value in the overall experience of your guests & players.

Helping Guests Who Ask For Directions

Always display a sincere helpful attitude when giving directions.

Showing restraint during confrontations & apprehensions

Professionalism is the key word! No guest wants to see a shouting match or a guest get beat up by security staff. Scenes like that can ruin a vacation for someone or traumatize some people.

You need to put on your acting face (and body language) during times of stress and frustration. Yep, even if you're dealing with a complete ding-bat, show them respect. Appreciate them. Their money helps pay the salaries for you and the other employees.

Read "Verbal Judo" by George Thompson, Phd. There are a couple versions printed. Read the original one first… the one geared towards law enforcement. Dr. Thompson does an excellent job of being realistic about the anger that we can feel when dealing with aggression on the job. He then gives very intelligent reasons for not taking things personal and deflecting insults, etc.

Never "get tricked" into a fight. Never let some jerk cause you to lose your job or get sued. If you have to put your hands on someone, make it fast and as quiet as possible. Follow the use of force continuum that your employer has trained you on.

Checking ID's

One of the basic functions that casino & night club security have in common is checking ID's of the patrons. The way a security officer goes about this can either be professional or can be crass & embarrassing to the patron.

The Approach

The approach should always be low key so that you don't draw 'an audience' to the scene. Smile, be polite, give the greeting of the day, introduce yourself, explain that you're just verifying id's tonight and ask the person how old they are. Of the underage people that sneak into the casino, over 50% will be honest about their age without you having to actually see their id.

If they answer with the legal age or above, thank them and tell them you just need to verify that on their ID and then you'll be on your way.

If they answer with an age that is younger than allowed, thank them for their honesty and quietly explain that due to state and federal laws, they'll be escorted off the property now.

The Request To Leave

This task is simple yet so many security personnel and bouncers make it difficult. "Asking" them to leave is the way to go. As a representative of the property owner, all you need to do is ask them to leave, inform them that you're trespassing them from the property and that they are not allowed to return (if applicable). When working a removal with a patron of the opposite sex, it helps to have another employee of the same gender as the patron witness the removal. This helps prevent or respond to false accusations involving sexual misconduct.

Sample Dialog From A Real Incident Report

Approaching two folks (one male & one female) that looked underage

Radio call to dispatch:
    Officer to control, ID check @ west entrance, 1 male – 1 female, over.

Dispatch:
    Thank you sir, good copy.

Round 1:

    Good evening folks, my name is Officer X and I work with the Casino. I'm doing some routine ID checks this evening and need to how old are.

Male

    I'm 19.

Officer

    Wonderful, and you ma'am?

Female

    I'm 17 but 18 in 2 weeks. (moving closer to officer and being very flirtatious)

Officer

    Ok, good deal. Excuse me for a moment.

Radio call to dispatch:

    Officer to control, we're all good over here – I'll be over there in a second for that 101. (This is a secret code phrase that means I'm about to remove someone, I need back-up, preferably with a female presence)

Officer

> Sorry about that. Ok, 19 & 17 – easy enough. I just need to see your ID's real quick for my activity log.

> Both hand their ID's over and officer jots down information. Simultaneously, back-up & female staff arrives and stands a bit away so that the persons being removed don't feel the presence.

Officer

> Here are your ID's back. Unfortunately, due to gaming laws & regulations, people under 18 are not allowed in the casino and people under 21 aren't allowed in the lounge… so I'll need you both to leave at this time.

Female

> Are you sure? I can make it worth your while. (as she begins to lean in)

Officer (smoothly steps off-side, not allowing her to close distance)

> This way please, the exit is over here. In addition to leaving tonight you won't be allowed back in which means I'm issuing you a trespass from our property.

(They're all walking toward the door)

Male

You're a fucking wanna-be pussy

Officer

Ahhhh, you've been talking to my ex-wife I see. (they reach the door) Have a safe night folks.

Two security officers follow the young couple to their car (from a distance) to ensure they leave without incident.

Points Learned From The Above Dialog

1. Be pleasant. Never just walk up and say "ID's… now"
2. Call for back-up using code phrases
3. Have opposite gender back-up present when possible. Not because it's required by law but because it helps you when defending false accusations.
4. Be polite after being insulted. Don't get tricked into an argument. They easily escalate into fights which escalate into

lawsuits ranging from excessive force to unlawful arrest to kidnapping.

5. Build supportive 3rd party witnesses by behaving professionally. Remember, in court – this is very important and time saving.

Assisting Guest / Players Who Speak Different Languages

Ok, anyone who has worked in security, customer service, etc. has probably dealt with someone they just can't understand. Whether it's in person, on the phone or a fellow employee. It can be very humorous. It can be very irritating.

ID Checks

Actually, checking ID's is a duty that officers in most assignments will have to do. As a matter of fact, many employees – not just security – will have to check ID's. It's a common yet **delicate** task when you take into consideration the public relations issues mentioned earlier in this course. So, remember – be professional, nice and consistent.

Here are some basics if checking ID's:

1. Ensure the picture on the profile matches the person who gave it to you.

a. Seems easy right? Many times it's not! I've checked ID's on people who had lost a lot of weight and they no longer resembled their picture at all.

b. Look at the nose, cheek bones, chin & ears.

2. Check the date. Is the ID valid?
3. Has it been altered in any way?
4. Picture swapped?
5. Date of Birth been smudged or typed over?
6. Is it counterfeit?

    a. Look at the watermarks or layered background that many states have.

7. Some ID are more difficult than others to reproduce.
8. Feel the ID.

    a. Do you notice any bubbling of laminate? Any cuts or slices in the edges?

Remember, some ID's may be real but in the hands of someone underage. Relatives ID's are often used by Youth so this makes it very challenging to determine face to photo recognition sometimes.

The State or Tribal Nation that your Casino is in may not have any laws that require a person to show you an ID. That's ok. As a property owner, the casino can make "showing a valid ID" a condition of admittance. If the person doesn't want to show you their ID…

that's ok. They'll just have to leave. Use the Trespass laws in your jurisdiction to legally warn and remove such person(s).

Logging each ID check should be a normal practice. If you're at a static post, you may have a sheet, iPad, etc. that your management wants you to complete for every ID check. If you're on a mobile patrol, you may have to call control / dispatch.

Either way, the date, time and number of people checked should be documented. This information helps prove to any inspector or auditor that the casino is meeting their legal requirements.

Confiscation = show time! This can go smooth or not. I've been in a few fights following an ID confiscation. Follow your casino's guidelines on this. People oftentimes have spent a lot of money on their fake ID's and when you take it… sometimes they go nuts! Just remember, it's not personal. Heck, I used to apologize when keeping someone's ID. A lot of officers say "never apologize for doing your job". Really? Why not? If it calms the situation down and allows me to (1) confiscate the ID and (2) remove the bad guy from the property without a fight (and/or excessive force lawsuit)… I don't see a problem with it.

I used to say things like:

> *"You're gonna hate me but according to state law, I have to keep this. I'm sorry, I used to be your age too, but I have to protect my employer and honestly… my job. I'm sorry if you lost money on this thing. Come on, walk with me."*

It worked like a charm in over 85% of my confiscations. No yelling or embarrassing the person who just got busted. Just professionally doing my job. I never lost 'face' or had an increase of people trying to 'get over on me' because I was a softy, etc.

Now – truth be told, I've always been in good shape and can handle myself due to my combatives training. This ability makes it easier to be nice, speak softly when the situation dictates and look people in the eye – and without saying it… letting them know you're ready to throw down if they make a wrong move.

Mobile Patrols

Hotel & guest rooms:

This assignment can be very interesting. You never know what you'll run into in a casino hotel. You'll experience very funny incidents and a few times in your career, you'll experience horrific assaults or maybe even a deadly incident.

A security officer patrolling the halls and common area of the hotel is looking for unauthorized people (people without key cards), illegal activities (prostitution & drug related activities), potential thief & burglar set-ups, assaults and other crime related incidents.

They'll also be on the lookout for fires, electrical and water damage issues. Yes – safety related issues are just as important as crime related issues.

Casino floor:

First priority is the physical safety of patrons and employees. The second priority is protecting the integrity of the gaming environment. In order to professionally achieve the two priorities, security management typically has two patrolling methods:

Assigning areas/beats to officers or assigning officers as roamers.

In the overwhelming majority of casinos, the use of Areas or Beats is the best method of coverage. Remember, even if you think you are a "superstar officer" and that you're the best roamer out there – the fact is that, most officers are average. Management has to create a system of security coverage that ensures the highest level of security with a staff of industry average staff. For that reason, assigning beats has shown to be the best way to manage casino security.

How should the casino floor be divided up? There are two basic items to use. The "Fire Escape Route Plan" (zoomed-out view of floor) and the "Slot Map" (zoomed-in view of smaller sections of floor). Management will have to really study the specific areas and activities within each area in order to determine how many officers will be used in staffing the casino floor.

Some of the activities to consider are:

1. Routine gaming:
    a. Table games
    b. Slot machines

2. Surrounding activities:
    a. Change booths
    b. Kiosks
    c. Restaurant entry ways
    d. Cash dispensing cages
    e. Mini-bars or alcohol storage areas

So, an officers' first priority is to patrol the area they were assigned. Second, they back-up other officers when needed. Finally, they switch back to their first priority after handling an unusual incident.

Your main tool of prevention is: engaging people. That means when you come across a person(s) whose behavior is out of place (specific to the environment), you need to stop and talk to them. Be relaxed and conversational. Identify them by checking their ID.

Most people who are up to no good will not have ID on them. At that point, you can ask them to leave the property due to the fact that it's casino policy that all patrons must be identifiable.

Let's say they have ID but - you did in fact interrupt a criminal plan. You may have made them nervous enough to halt their plan and leave. Observe their body language and mannerisms. Have you detected any signs of discomfort? These will be important for you to make note of.

Restrooms

Patrolling restrooms is a **must**. The bad guys know about CCTV not being allowed inside of restrooms and they take advantage of it.

From rapes and molestation to robbery and drug deals… restrooms can be a scary place. There are criminals who work alone that target restrooms and there are teams and gangs that work them.

Imagine walking into a restroom and being assault as you're sitting on the toilet. It's happened many times.

Imagine sitting on the toilet and having someone reach over and steal your jacket or purse off the hook. That happens too.

Consistent patrolling is irritating to the criminal element. The goal is to have them think that any score they may get… just isn't worth all the hassle that your security program gives them.

Garages & parking lots

This assignment, when done correctly, can save a casino huge amount of money on an annual basis. Thefts, rapes, assaults, prostitution, drug related activities, car accidents, burglaries, robberies, stolen cars, vehicle damage and other crimes all have occurred or been planned in the garages and parking lots of casinos. Oh, let's not forget fraudulent claims of the above crimes happening that end up in court or early settlements.

These areas can be very difficult to protect due to the many access points. Vehicle entry and exits, property walkways and finally - elevators into & out of the casino-hotels.

Having a security officer who is truly engaged and focused on crime prevention is a true asset. Having an officer who is lazy, asleep at the wheel or assigned to this task as a punishment – is a horrible situation.

Now that we've covered the crimes that occur in garages let's cover the most frequent calls for service that we discovered in casino (and hospital) parking lots & garages:

1. Can you help me find my car?
2. Can you jump start my dead battery?
3. Surveillance needs you to check a vehicle out - there appears to be a couple having sex in the vehicle.
4. Can you help this guy? He locked himself out of his car.
5. Can you check on some kids left in a car?
6. Surveillance reported a local "repossession company" hooking up a vehicle.

All Patrol Assignments – Checking Trash Containers

Casino security and loss prevention from many industries have learned how valuable checking trash containers is to securing their property and/or business.

Bad guys can be casino players, hotel guests or people who just wander onto the property. It's very common for purse and wallet snatchers to take the money and credit cards… and then dump the purse & wallets in the trash.

Some bad guys are actually staff, contractors & vendors. They often place items that they want to steal in a trash can or dumpster. This way they can (1) buy a little time to get over their nerves (2) see if the items are reported as stolen or (3) test the reporting delay for a future theft.

On a less devious note but still un-allowed, security often finds empty bottles and cans from staff who drink alcohol on duty.

Fixed Posts

Dispatcher

Probably one of the most underestimated jobs in security. (corrections or law enforcement for that matter). This position should be filled by a quick thinker. Someone who works confidently with a computer and can learn to multi-task quickly.

There have been many officers who thought they were God's gift to the industry until they had to endure a shift as dispatcher. They panicked, became stressed and angry because they couldn't deal with the incoming calls, alarms and requests.

Multi-screen computer displays, intricate phone systems, multi-channel base station and handheld radios along with an electronic blotter (log book) are common items for a dispatcher.

Lost and Found

Normally a more relaxed job, however an important one. Great customer service and displayed empathy are two of many attributes needed here. Combine those with an ability to make log entries of items as they are brought in or claimed, and you'll be all set.

Ingress & Egress locations - Employee entrances & loading docks

Entrances and exits for both patrons and staff need to be manned. Management of these positions is so important. Officers should be given breaks every other hour for the restroom or to get a quick bite to eat.

Keep the officers fed, check on them via radio & welfare checks and allow them to move around a bit. This job is well known for aches & pains and hungry stomachs combined with long periods of boredom.

Stay alert and stay sharp. Being well rested is so important when assigned here. Working on the casino floor tends to have enough energy, action and adrenaline dumps throughout a shift that even a tired officer can have his/her day fly buy. But if you're working a static post with nothing going on… the sleep monster can get you.

Body Language & Player Evaluation

This is going to be one of the most amazing skill sets you pick up while working in the casino. Rule # 1 – there are no hard-n-fast rules for body language. For example, I read in one book that people with their arms crossed are being defensive and lying. This isn't always true. Another book mentioned that people who walk into a casino and aren't smiling are up to no good. Not always true.

Here's the best advice. First, if one isn't assigned to you… find a mentor and learn from this person. The casino has a different heartbeat than all other areas of security. Regardless of your background… you'll be a "newbie in training" for a while and you need to be ok with this. Many former law enforcement and military folks hate hearing that, but they need to get over it. Their background means they'll learn a lot faster than most, but it doesn't mean they're already qualified to work the floor alone.

Second, set the immediate assumptions of lying, up to no good, etc. aside. Here's the way a professional casino security officer looks at the environment and people.

1. They learn the baseline behaviors of people as they enter, play and/or work in the environment they're assigned to.

2. Then they adopt these three labels into their vocabulary: 'comfort', 'discomfort' and 'out of the ordinary'.

When the professional security officer sees a person showing signs of discomfort or behaving in a manner that is out of the ordinary... they investigate. They study from a distance and gather more information. They DON'T overreact, get all amped up and harass the person. They get curious and actively look into the situation.

Here are tasks involving the above:

1. Watching people as they enter the casino
2. Watching people in the garages and parking lots
3. Watching people as they play games
4. Watching and listening to them during interviews and investigations
    a. people = patrons & staff
5. When dealing with the human element, security staff needs to be intelligently assertive... NOT aggressive.
6. When dealing with the security management program as a whole – it needs to aggressively deter and/or recognize dangerous or criminal situations.

Bouncer Duty (trespassing & removing people)

Minors, Drunks, Attempted Thieves, etc. – at one time or another you'll have to eject these and other people from the property. This task needs to be done very professionally. Never engage in shouting and cursing matches. Never behave in a manner that if overheard by a by-stander or observed on CCTV… would appear to be a mutual fight.

At the beginning of each shift, officers should check the blacklist. (also known as the '86 list' or 'trespass list') This will inform the officer of people who have been placed on the 'not allowed back on property' list since they worked last.

Just like a police officer takes verbal abuse… so does the casino security officer. Don't take it personally. Remember, you have the authority and last act. So if the bad guy wants to run his/her mouth… just remember to document everything when you write your report. Always keep your cool – even while restraining someone.

Seeing a fight can be very traumatic for a bystander so don't add to it by adding bravado statements and beating someone up because "they deserved it". That behavior can you fired and both you and the casino sued.

In addition, remember that the person who's arguing with you could be a future customer or a friend / family member of one of your biggest players. It's for that reason these incidents need to be handled professionally.

The Use of Force Policy & Supervisor's Discretion

These items are something that all officers need to be aware of. The use of force policy will cover when officers should go from (1) verbal demands to (2) compelled movement to (3) control holds to (4) defensive tactics, etc.

Many casinos are now using the 3 fingers technique. (Read "Casino Security and Gaming Surveillance Handbook" for detailed info) This is a 3 warning system where after each warning the primary officer holds his hand in the air with 1, 2 or 3 fingers in the air. The number of fingers tells his back-up and the surveillance room what step of the process he's in. Once he holds up 3 fingers, the back-up moves in for the escort or restraint.

Now, let's address the Supervisors Discretion. Even if a Casino has a 3 finger system in place… the supervisor has discretion to step in and give the person a dozen chances if he/she deems reasonable. Why? Because every situation is different and the reasons listed above for remaining professional come into play.

This may be called a "hand off" in some casinos. Remember, if your boss elects to spend extra time "working a guy" and gives him more chances before going hand on… that's not a slam or disrespect towards you. It's your boss trying to prevent a situation from escalating at the current moment **and** days later with legal or damaged reputation issues.

What door do you send them to? Should you escort them to the door or all the way to their vehicle? Your employer's policy should cover this. However, remember – this isn't TV or the movies. We don't launch people out the front door on their faces and then close the door. That creates an angry patron who can do a lot of damage between the casino door and their vehicle. They may damage property or harm innocent people.

The task of removing undesirables is a perfect one for insisting that all officers maintain their physical fitness. Whatever your natural size, develop your pound-for-pound strength and practice defensive tactics frequently. Don't wait for your employer to send you to initial or refresher training… take this responsibility on yourself. Maintain your skills. Supervisors & managers – you need to ensure your employees are trained.

Plain Clothes Assignments

Ok, these are just plain fun! Whether you're undercover working as a "player", assigned with someone of the opposite gender pulling 'couple duty' or hiding in a bathroom stall listening for drug and prostitution deals or assaults to occur... this is a nice change up in your security career.

Plain clothes stings are very effective – especially once the word gets out that your casino employs this tactic. Why? The bad guys will eventually go to an easier target. (another casino) The reason why you don't see this type of assignment more frequently comes down to the budget. A lot of times paying for extra officers is just cost prohibitive.

Critical Area Security

What are critical areas?

- Military – Weapons room & ammo points
- Pharmaceutical manufacturer – Controlled substance cages & coolers
- Bodyguard work – VIP's hotel room
- Casino – (1) Vault; (2) Cashier cage; (3) Fill and box drop routes (4) areas of unusual concern and more

These areas will demand more officers, more surveillance and plain clothes work. We have two goals here. 1st – beef up the security. 2nd – give the perception that there is much more security than there really is. As mentioned earlier in the course – security done well will persuade the bad guys to go look for another victim property. Why? Because you have "hardened the target" so much that it's too much trouble to mess with your casino.

Training the Security Officer

A professional security operation will have a structured training program. It doesn't matter if the new employee is a former secret service agent, navy seal or seasoned pro from a different property. We're talking about operational consistency, vicarious liability and enhanced professionalism.

If someone thinks they're 'above training' – they need to be terminated. A professional knows that even if they've been trained on a certain task before… that refresher training will make them sharper.

In addition, the majority of all skill sets are perishable. So, a training program should consist of:

(1) N.E.O. Training (New Employee Orientation)
(2) Basic Security Officer Training
       Dept Specific Orientation

Entry level surveillance room
Gaming area observation
Hotel & guest room

(3) Advanced Officer Training
Offsite client protection
Supervisor training
Instructor development

(4) Annual refresher training
Casino wide topics
Security specific

Surveillance Operations

Role of the surveillance officer / department

"The more we detect, the more we prevent. The more we prevent, the more revenue our casino will realize."

In a perfect world, we'd have physical security presence on the ground and CCTV coverage everywhere! Unfortunately, budgets just won't allow for that… and in cases where the budget is big enough… there are laws that prevent it. (Bathrooms, guest rooms, etc.)

Here are 4 basic rules:

(1) Put officers & cameras everywhere you can

(2) Put officers where you can't have cameras

(3) Put cameras where you can't have officers

(4) Have a structured CCTV training system in place for officers

Once we've done the above, the surveillance department mission can be broken down into these four goals: Enhance, detect, inform and report.

Enhance

Surveillance departments enhance the observational presence & reporting accuracy of the security officers.

Detect

Surveillance departments detect attempted or actual criminal acts, violations of policy, etc. when security officers of other staff are not in the area.

Inform

Surveillance officers inform security officers of un-allowed incidents so that security can respond promptly. They can also 'follow' suspects and feed real-time information to the responding officers. Finally, they can inform responding security of any traps the bad guys have waiting for them. Having an 'eye-in-the-sky' is an invaluable tool for management. Sometimes the CCTV Feeds reveal a larger problem and the chase will be called off so that no further injuries or financial loss occurs.

Report / Record

The surveillance officer does the reporting and the system does the recording... simple as that.

Assignments (functions) within casino

Surveillance Patrol – IOU Patrol

As a surveillance officer, you'll be assigned to patrol a certain area of the property. A very effective type of patrol that has been taught for many years in the industry is the I.O.U. patrol. It stands for identify, observe and understand.

Identify

Identify all persons involved in the activity you're concerned with AND those in the immediate area.

Observe

Observe the policy violations, criminal activity (preparations & set-ups), cheating or advantage play. You may be observing a back entrance, hallway, gaming table, slot machine, etc. You'll be watching for physical behaviors & mannerisms to bets being waged, to game strategy. There is so much to be observed!

Understand

Understanding what you're looking at is the final element. Is the employee at the back dock handling a routine task or are they there at a different time of day and not acting normal?

Is the player cheating? Is the player using legal yet unwanted 'advantage play'?

Is what you're looking at suspicious - in any way?

Everything from employees skimming tills to players cheating to violent criminals stalking their next victims near the restrooms can be detected on CCTV.

Conduct Surveillance Audits

This is something I first participated in while working in adult and juvenile corrections. We used audits to gather info on gang activity and improper employee-inmate relationships.

I was happy when I learned Casino's do the same thing. Well, some Casino's do. A lot still don't and that is a shame.

Difference between 'monitoring' & 'auditing'?

Monitoring is more re-active. When staff is monitoring the cameras, they're looking for ANYTHING that catches their eye. Auditing is very proactive. When staff is auditing an area, they're looking for SPECIFIC activity based on information & instructions that were given to them by management.

The big 3 things they would be looking for are:

(1) Criminal activity
(2) Suspicious activity
(3) Not following rules, policies & procedures

Areas To Consider Auditing Are Determined By:

- Operating statistics
- Crime trends

- Exception reports
- Violations of internal controls, policies, procedures, etc.

Each Audit Has A Case File:

Your management will tell you exactly what they want placed in the file. Remember, an audit is looking for specific information. If you detect something that is worthy of further investigation, document it somewhere else and bring it to your supervisors' attention. (This info is important and, in many cases, will justify a Surveillance Close Watch. See below)

Casino Floor:

- Main Cage
- Slot Jackpots & Fills
- Table Game Player Rating Cards
- Credit or Marker Transactions

Other Areas: (Finding things here will get employees talking!)

- Bar Till(s)
  - Staff stealing; no receipts; etc

- Drink Stations
  - Staff making drinks for themselves / friends without paying

- Restaurant Cashier
  - Staff not charging family & friends

- Food Prep Areas
  - Staff preparing & eating food without paying

- Loading Docks
  - Theft, other crimes or unsafe work practices

Surveillance Close Watch

Many times, the surveillance department will come across information that leads towards suspicious information aimed at a specific Person or Area. When that occurs, management may initiate a Close Watch on that person or area.

Close Watch On Person:

The assigned surveillance officer will follow the person for the entire shift… for as many days as they are told to. The officer will document this person's activities and share with management.

Close Watch On Area:

The assigned surveillance officer will monitor **all activities** the area for the entire shift… for as many days as they are told to. The officer will document this area's activities and share with management.

Only the best officers should be assigned to these. Why? Because this duty can get boring and an amateur officer will become less attentive. The officer needs patience and should truly believe in the value of this task. No observation is too small. Nothing should be taken lightly.

Basic Camera Skills

Tri Shot Coverage

In casinos, this is easier to accomplish because they often have a larger budget and will invest in more cameras per area. For example – they may have 3 individual cameras in place to record the Tri-shots listed below.

In other security operations and corrections facilities, the budgets are smaller. Thus, the officer has to achieve the Tri-shot by zooming in & out, panning and taking 'snap shots' when appropriate.

A tri-shot is simply recording these 3 things: An overview; a specific shot; and an ID shot. Let's look at each:

(1) Overview of Activity

> Front of house example:
>
>> Blackjack Table: Dealers cards, players cards, card shoe, shuffler, players hands, entire table plus people around table.
>
> Back of house example:
>
>> Loading Dock: Includes the dock floor, large delivery door, small man door and a lot of floor space.

(2) Specific Shot

> Front of house example:
>
>> Blackjack Table: Close up on players hands showing him manipulating cards.
>
> Back of house example:

Loading Dock: Close up of an employee taking one box per pallet and setting it off to the side. Another employee takes box and leaves building with it.

(3) ID Shot

Front of house example:

Blackjack Table: Close up on players face

Back of house example:

Loading Dock: Close up on both employees faces

Plain view & Hidden Camera Placement

Plain view cameras deter a lot of criminal and unwanted activity. However, the creative bad guys out there work around them. Thus, we have a need for hidden cameras.

Once a bad guy is caught or employees are busted & terminated via evidence recorded on hidden cameras… the word spreads FAST. Sure, people get upset about Big Brother, but that's what saves the casino money and keeps the honest employees earning money!

A word of caution: Before placing hidden cameras, get approval from the corporate legal department. The legal dept looks at two issues at a minimum:

(1) Is placing hidden cameras legal in the federal, state, province, tribal area.

(2) If so, is the crime you're trying to detect worth all the "hidden camera legal claims" that will occur if this goes to court.

> ie. Using hidden cameras in a private office to catch an employee sleeping isn't normally worth the backlash. Using hidden cameras to detect the sales of narcotics, meth, etc. in a private office is worth the backlash.

People have a "reasonable expectation of privacy" in many areas so the legal dept will look into this as well.

Game Observation Skills

This is where consistent training comes into play. Every system is different and to make it more challenging, systems are often layered. Meaning you can login to a secure intranet to access the cameras AND login via a remote connection on the internet.

The internet and intranet functionalities are different in many cases. Sure, the salesman who sold you on the system may swear that there won't be any difference… but take it from me (someone who has years of experience behind the cameras…) there is always a difference.

(1) Know the surveillance equipment and practice the infrequent tasks during slow times.

(2) Know the games. Attend training seminars, read books on how to play & win.

(3) Know the game specific cons. Read books on how to cheat, etc. Find videos online of people bragging about their cons.

(4) Know player "money management". This education will come from your time at work, your mentor and your off work studying. Wealthy & intelligent players who play LEGALLY will cost a casino more than most people think. Learn by watching these folks!

(5) Be proactive – Study, develop a healthy paranoia and go get'm!

Employee pilferage and other Crimes from within

One of the disappointing realities of owning a business is that some employees steal. This hurts the business revenue, the wages of all employees, bonus opportunities, etc.

Watching staff isn't an issue of "Big Brother Not Trusting" it's a matter of historical fact. Like it or not, it's a reality. I've always had an open attitude toward unannounced drug tests I've had to do or having my bags searched, etc. Why? Because I understand that all business lose money. Whether the criminal employee(s) is from Security, Surveillance. The Bar, or a Dealer… losses have occurred.

Use the Surveillance Close Watch to discover any of these losses in your casino!

Con Games & Scams

Slip and Fall Con:

Slip and fall cons have been discovered over & over! Employees, players and hotel guests have all scored huge amounts of money in scams like this.

Methods of cheating by players:

Past Posting:

After a bet is won, one replaces smaller-denomination chips with large-denomination chips.

Hand Mucking:

Palming desirable cards, then switching them for less desirable cards that the gambler holds.

Marking Cards:

During play, there are various methods for doing this. Study your craft and learn how this is done by **observing**.

Introducing Previously Marked Decks Into Play:

Usually involves "inside" help, i.e., the collusion of casino employees. There are many different ways to mark decks of cards, some of them very difficult to detect.

False Deals:

> Ability to deal the second card from the top (used in conjunction with marked cards), or the ability to deal the bottom card of the deck (used in conjunction with placing desirable cards at the bottom of the deck.)

False Shuffles and Cuts:

> Ability to seemingly mix and cut the cards while retaining certain cards or the whole deck in a desired order.

Shuffling Machines:

> Various arraignments of the cards.

Slot Machines:

> Stringing; Wands; etc. Many methods exist for altering the outcome of slot machine games.

Collusion:

> In poker games, the practice of two partners signaling to each other the values of their cards; this can be very

difficult to detect. There is also such a phenomenon as dealer cheating at gambling world: a player bribes a dealer and they share the winning after the game. Though this method is rather risky for dealers, some of them do not mind taking part in it.

Using Auxiliary Devices (in Nevada, USA for example):

In Nevada casinos, using any device which helps to forecast the odds or aid in a legitimate strategy such as card counting is regarded as cheating; such devices have been outlawed due to the unique ability of Nevada's large gambling industry to influence legislation. Auxiliary devices are not generally regarded as cheating and can be increasingly difficult to detect as electronic aids become smaller and easier to hide.

Top Hat:

In Roulette, players place a bet after the ball has landed. The chips are disguised using a third party's chip - the top hat.

Incident Management

Minor

Most casinos will have a Standard Operating Procedure for minor incidents. Follow your policy! Minor incidents are things like:

- Calls involving drunk people
- Verbal arguments
- Fist fights
- Domestic violence arguments and fights

Steps To Manage:

- Notify dispatch of incident & request back-up if needed
- Surveillance overhears call & moves cameras over to area for recording.
- Move un-involved patrons away from incident
- Intervene when it's best to do so (Be smart, wait for back-up)
- Remove the involved parties from the property when necessary.

Major

Most casinos will have a Standard Operating Procedure for major incidents. Follow your policy! Major incidents are things like:

- Robbery
- Fire
- Active shooter
- Full power outages

An emergency preparedness plan is something every casino should have. Good points of contact for helping with your plan are:

- Property insurance inspector
- Fire Department Business Inspector
- Police Department Community Officer
- Government anti-terror websites & sample plans
- Industry specific consultants.

Investigations

What Is Investigation?

Investigation is the process of inquiry that helps uncover what happened in an incident. Casino security / management conduct investigations to find out the truth behind an allegation and whether there is evidence of a criminal offense being committed.

What Happens During Investigations?

During investigations, security may conduct interviews to obtain details of the case. What is told by the witness to the security during the interview(s) may be recorded in a Police statement at a later time.

Where Can A Statement Be Taken / Recorded?

A statement is usually taken in an interview room. However, security may also record statements at the scene of crime or in some cases, at a place convenient to the person who is being interviewed.

What If A Person Refuses To Be Interviewed?

Contact your supervisor or legal counsel.

Who Can Be Called Up For Investigations?

Anyone whom you believe has knowledge of the facts of the case may be called up for investigations. The length of the interview would depend on the nature of the case and how much information you require from the person being interviewed. It also depends on how long the person is willing to give you.

Ten Steps For Investigations:

Inform management and/or legal department of the investigation. Get approvals when needed. Remember – we're private security **not** law enforcement. Law enforcement can be a very good team member when the lines of communication are kept open & healthy.

1. Prepare case files
2. Question witnesses and victims and gather data
3. Process evidence
4. Develop informants
5. Interrogate suspects
6. Conduct background investigations
7. Conduct surveillance
8. Prepare and maintain detailed records
9. Inform law enforcement
10. Testify in court if needed

Conclusion

Be smart! Remember, patron safety is more important than arresting a robber sometimes. In December 2010, the Bellagio in Las Vegas was the victim of a robbery. They decided to let the armed bad guy go. They made the right decision.

Chapter 6: Conclusion

Change is the law of life. And those who look only to the past or present are certain to miss the future.
~John F. Kennedy

Let's wrap this book up! In the first part, we focused on the human being. First, you - the security specialist and second, the people you'll come into contact with. We explained that we feel this is the most important area to focus on when someone tells us they want to perform and be recognized in Top 10 Percent of the industry. We hope that is your goal!

We also explained that this industry is very competitive. There are many people with military and law enforcement backgrounds who are competing for high level jobs and/or contracts. The majority have great looking resumes and career experience. The "soft skills" are what will propel you – above them – when everything else is equal.

So, learn about yourself, other people, and communication in part one! Remember, humans have two ears and only one mouth. Reflect on that.

The second part of the book covered two aspects of security. First, the industry as a whole. We looked at the fundamentals of physical security and identified numerous tools you can use to keep your company or client as safe as possible. Second, we focused in on the world of casino security. The hope is that you'll be able to see the tools discussed in part one – being applied to the casino industry. We chose the casino security arena because of how complex it is.

There was some overlapping of topics in the two parts. This was intentional. Now it's your turn. Take action on the information you've read. Success awaits you! *~ End ~*

Would You Mind Leaving A Review?

After reading this book, if you find that the information shared is what was promised in the Table of Contents… please leave a review on Amazon.com & Barnes and Noble. Thank you!

Resources

Since the memorization and applicable skills of the material in this book are perishable, I highly recommend you study books, dvd's or attend seminars by the following people:

1. Joe Navarro
2. Derek Banas
3. Steven Van Aperen
4. George Thompson, PhD

In addition to the above, study these books:

5. Body Language for Dummies
6. Body Language 101, David Lambert
7. Casino Security and Gaming Surveillance Handbook
8. Adventures In Casino Security
9. Casino Surveillance and Security: 150 Things You Should Know

Finally, join the **American Society for Industrial Security**!

Invest MONEY in the products of the people mentioned above! I have! I feel they are amazing instructors & authors!

About the Author

Brian K. Allen has worked in the field of professional security for over 25 years. From line security officer, supervisor of safety & security, US Army military policeman, bouncer, executive protection specialist, and currently as Director of International Security Training, LLC. (based out of Mesa, Arizona - USA), Brian has "been there done that" in this industry.

When not working, Brian enjoys powerlifting and studying and teaching martial arts.

Online Courses Available

Interested in furthering / refreshing your education in the professional security industry? If so, International Security Training, LLC. can help you do just that! Whether you're trying to update a few resume lines or beef up some marketing material for your business, International Security Training, LLC. has a course or actually… many courses that will help.

Since 2003 they've been helping students & peers alike! Visit their website today!

InternationalSecurityTraining.org

Made in the USA
Las Vegas, NV
18 October 2024